HARNESS THE
POWER
OF PERSONAL BRANDING
AND EXECUTIVE PRESENCE

HARNESS THE
POWER
OF PERSONAL BRANDING
AND EXECUTIVE PRESENCE

ELEVATE YOUR LIFE AND CAREER–NOW!

S. RENEE SMITH

For general information on our other products and services, please contact S. Renee Smith within the U.S. at 888-588-0423 or srenee@srenee.com.

Books by S. Renee Smith are published in a variety of electronic and print formats. Some content that appears in print may not be available in electronic books, and vice versa.

TRADEMARKS: There Is More Inside logo is a registered trademark of S. Renee Smith, and may not be used without written permission.

ISBN: Print 978-1-7330219-0-6   eBook 978-1-7330219-1-3

S. RENEE'S
There Is More Inside

*To my husband, HL Larry. You came into my life at the perfect time;
your love and encouragement leave me speechless.*

*To my parents, William J. & Shirley M. Smith, Sr. By example,
you've shown me what it takes to build a respectable brand.
With your support, you've helped me sustain it.*

*To my readers, clients, fans, and followers, you help my brand breathe;
now, I want to help yours do the same.*

Additional Titles by S. Renee

There Is More Inside: Personal Essentials Needed to Living a Power-Packed Life

The Bridge to Your Brand: Likability, Marketability, Credibility

Our Hearts Wonder: Prayers to Heal Your Heart and Calm Your Soul

Self-Esteem for Dummies

*5 Steps to Assertiveness: How to Communicate with Confidence
and Get What You Want*

CONTENTS

INTRODUCTION

YOU ARE A POWERFUL LEADER, AND YOU KNOW IT.
However, it happened again. You were passed over for the promotion or slighted for the contract. You've invested time and money in your education and professional growth. Each day you give your best, and you're committed to outstanding work performance. Still, the people who you want to notice you—don't. They are not putting two and two together; you're the person they need.

It's discouraging and frustrating when leadership doesn't recognize the value of your work. Moreover, it's disheartening when your personal brand isn't compelling enough to build your business. Feeling stuck, you begin to question yourself and wonder whether you're as good as you think. "What am I doing wrong? Why can't people see how hard I work and how talented I am? Will I ever get to the next level?"

You are dynamic and talented, and I want to help you level the playing field by increasing the probability that future opportunities will lean in your favor. You can speak up and overcome any reason not to stand out. People should acknowledge and respect who you are and what you do. You have the right to ask for what you want and to get what you've earned. There's one big problem: You don't know how.

I'm S. Renee, and at 12 years old I learned that success comes to those who are best able to communicate who they are and their value. Back then, I was seeking to escape from being bullied. After determining who I wanted to be, which meant living by my values, within two years of practicing the foundational principles I share with you in this book, the student body of my middle school voted me "Queen" and "most popular, friendliest, and most reliable." Do you want respect, admiration, and recognition? The formula still works today.

I've been fortunate to work as a corporate marketing representative; model and actress; television talk show host, producer, and spokesperson for the United Paramount Network in Philadelphia; director of public relations at an academic institution; and a retail manager. Since the launch of my speaking and writing career in 2005, I've taught my branding and executive presence models at colleges and universities, corporations, state and government agencies, and nonprofits.

Through presentations and coaching people of various ages, walks of life, and income levels, I've helped hundreds of thousands of people around the world become workplace and industry influencers, elevate their careers, and yes, even improve personal relationships. I've built my brand from being an unknown in the self-development industry to becoming a nationally recognized self-esteem, branding, and communication expert—writing and releasing three books and signing two book deals in the process. Even as an established professional in the marketplace, roughly every three years, I reexamine my brand to ensure I haven't outgrown it and that my message is still relevant to my audiences.

By completing this personal growth process, you'll discover the joy of becoming more of yourself, and you'll cherish the perks of being a likable, marketable, and credible commodity. I give you the steps you'll need to package, position, and promote yourself without appearing boastful and the tools to equip yourself to navigate problematic situations and perplexing cultures. You'll also gain confidence in how to connect and communicate with various audiences, including executives.

It's going to take effort though. Building a recognizable brand requires contemplation, commitment, and consistency. I'll give you the strategies, but you'll have to implement them. More importantly, you have to live the brand you design for yourself and deliver according to its promise. I believe that real stories, practical advice, and an easy-to-follow blueprint to building your brand and executive presence will give you the conviction and courage to accomplish your goals.

Building a notable brand creates a buzz about your professional expertise, and executive presence sets you up to become the go-to person in the industry you work. Of more considerable significance, living your brand gives you clarity of purpose and raises your credibility among the people your brand reaches. When those individuals experience your brand and witness your executive presence, they want to be like you—making you a role model for authentic success. I've given this process much thought over the years, and I've refined it to these three, easy-to-follow steps:

1. Package Your Brand and Develop Executive Presence
2. Position Your Brand and Practice Executive Presence
3. Promote Your Brand and Present Executive Presence

You deserve a seat at the table. It's your turn to be called the expert. I intend to give you the information and inspiration to manage your mental barriers and to put you on a path toward achieving the success you've held close to your heart—a hope you may have never had the courage to express. This process is tested and proven to yield results. Testimonies confirm that it's insightful and useful. As you turn each page, I hope to challenge, guide, prompt, and inspire you. Are you ready to get people talking about you? Then let's get started.

PART ONE
BRANDING BASICS

The phone rang.

"Hi, Ms. Smith. This is Andrew. I did an internship with you several years ago. I'm applying for law school and was wondering if you would write a letter of recommendation for me." I calmly responded, "Congratulations, Andrew, on pursuing a law degree. The last time we spoke, you told me you were behind in your studies and couldn't complete your tasks on time. You requested that I give you a passing grade and, in turn, you promised to complete your responsibilities after your exams. In good faith, I agreed. Andrew, I held up my end of our deal, but I never heard from you again until now. For that reason, I'm not comfortable writing a letter of recommendation for you."

He apologized. I accepted his apology, but it was too late. He was branded.

Everyone has a brand. You may never know why a person doesn't respond to you positively, but there's something about what you did, how you did it, and what you communicated to them that made them feel uncertain about you. It may not be as apparent as the college graduate who was shamefully dishonorable, yet even subtle messages you convey can create barriers to relationships and career advancement.

Your everyday habits could be the behaviors that are making a negative impression on leaders without you even knowing it—and no one is willing to tell you. I've been hired by organizations to address issues such as email etiquette, what's appropriate to wear to work, how to effectively communicate, nonverbal cues that make you appear clueless, and what to say when you don't know what to say.

Let's be clear, you've heard it before: Your first impression is critically important. What you may not have heard is that every interaction after that is equally crucial. No impression is carved in stone. Building a bankable brand requires consistent performance. People won't feel safe with you if they don't know what to expect from you.

In Part One, I help you identify mental hurdles that cause you to talk yourself out of pursuing your ambitions. I provide exercises throughout this book that I call "Mind Elevation." They are designed to move you forward by raising your level of self-awareness and confidence. As you complete each Mind Elevation, you'll begin to notice your vision of yourself expanding and your brand forming.

In this section, I walk you through overcoming uncertainty and give you the tools you need to silence doubt by developing a mindset for greater success. You'll also become clear about people's perceptions of you and identify ways to transform and transcend areas of your brand that are blocking your progress.

Part Two is the brand and executive presence development process presented in three steps: creating your brand package and developing brand presence, deciding how you'll position your brand within an organization or industry while learning how to master yourself, and developing a promotional strategy and presenting as an executive.

If you follow the process I lay out for you in these pages, you'll be able to declare, without hesitation, who you are and what you do, and proclaim your value in a non-threatening, clear, and concise way.

I strongly suggest you use a journal or notebook to keep all your notes, thoughts, and mind elevation responses in one place as you work through this book, or you could purchase my corresponding workbook at srenee.com. Let's begin the process by identifying your perceptions of branding. Write your responses to the questions below. Then start reading Chapter 1.

1. What is a brand?
2. What is my current brand?
3. What does it mean to have executive presence?
4. Do I have executive presence?
5. What do I do that indicates I have executive presence?
6. How do people feel when they leave my presence?
7. When I'm not around, what do people say about me?

CHAPTER 1
MINDSET SHIFT

WEEK AFTER WEEK, we'd meet to create a strategy of how to redesign her brand. At the end of each session, she'd excitedly confirm her task for the week to advance development of her brand and to begin testing the effectiveness of the work we had completed. Although she had good intentions, there was a problem: She became paralyzed when it was time to act.

Does that sound like you? You know what you want, but you feel stuck. You blame the lack of forward movement on being too busy or unclear about what to do. You know that, fundamentally, you're afraid of rejection or making a mistake. You may even be asking yourself, "Who am I to want that promotion or contract?"

You answer yourself by reasoning within yourself, that you don't have enough experience, or that there are people who are much more qualified than you. You then seek the opinion of people who will not hold you accountable to the bigger vision you have for yourself. Nevertheless, you say you're looking for that next opportunity to advance in your business or career. Making progress in achieving what you want begins with asking yourself this question: "Do I want it or not?"

Here's how a client describes what happened when I asked her that question:

When S. Renee scolded me during a coaching consult, I was shocked to come face-to-face with the excuses I was giving myself to justify being stuck. She was right. Did I want to sell my products or not? In the wake of that event, I committed to moving forward and stop wasting her time and mine. That was a big wake-up call for me, for which I am very thankful.

I was confused by the assertion that I had "scolded her." However, I'm always thrilled to receive updates regarding my clients' accomplishments. Yes, guiding her to the right path is another success story for my brand, but of grander significance is the mindset pivot that led to her success.

I don't need a case study to know that for any brand to thrive, a person must first have the right mindset. To get what you want, you have to be competent and confident about who you are, what you do, and the results you deliver.

In this chapter, you'll learn where doubt originates and how to dissolve it.

A Mental Leap

My husband tells me frequently, "You're comfortable with asking questions that make people uncomfortable." I never knew that about myself, and it's never my intention to make a person uncomfortable. Whether I'm in the presence of an individual or group, I want to inspire them to grasp what's inside them. That requires attentive, compassionate listening so that I can ask the right questions to help them move from discomfort to see greater possibilities for themselves.

Most often, I only have a small window of opportunity to pinpoint where a person is in their life, where they want to go, and how to help them get there. Assisting clients requires hearing what they're saying and not saying. Then I can coach them through their mental blocks to seeing their capacity for success. However, I had to help myself do this first.

I remember when I received the call in 2014 to consider co-authoring, *Self-Esteem for Dummies*. I couldn't believe it. Me? Really? Wiley? Wiley is one of the top publishers in the world, "Do I have the writing ability to meet their standards? I'm not on that level," I thought. Being fired from a job 15 years earlier for allegedly being a poor writer didn't help my confidence. All the negative emotions within me surged from the place where I had suppressed them. Have you ever noticed that past hurts often haunt us at a time when our past successes should empower us?

At the time of the call, I had produced two self-published books and had been on the speaking circuit for nearly a decade. I was being hired to develop and present many self-development programs for organizations, coach hundreds of one-on-one clients, share national platforms with international leaders, and give advice to the readers and viewers of media outlets. My measurable results for clients were indisputable, plus a 98 percent return-customer rate made my brand credible. Still, I didn't think I was qualified to write for the world's best-selling reference brand series.

The thought of putting my writing under a microscope for industry experts to judge made me feel vulnerable. As I battled these demons, I secretly wanted to accept the opportunity. For weeks, I kept everyone connected to the project at bay as I strategically asked people who knew nothing about writing or publishing if I should accept the project. I would set up the conversation so it would affect their thinking, then nudge them toward advising me to avoid signing the contract. I hit the bullseye nearly every time—except when I asked my father. He didn't take the bait. My "executive coach," who never graduated high school, said, "I don't know enough about the business to advise you on this, but if you decide to do it, you'll do a great job." I took that as a yes.

The last person I called was a friend in the book-marketing business, Steve Harrison. He had promoted *Chicken Soup for the Soul, Rich Dad Poor Dad*, and other notable titles. He had hired me to coach his clients in brand development and speaking. When I approached him, I didn't want him to see my insecurities, so I focused on the facts. He advised me that I'd gain added credibility from writing for Wiley, and more projects could come my way once the book was published. I couldn't argue with anything he said. He confirmed what I already knew.

Have you ever been in that situation? You want to go to the next level, and an opportunity has been extended to you to get there, but fear paralyzes you? Despite my doubts, I decided to move forward. The book's co-author and I submitted the requested writing sample separately. After reviewing our submissions, the acquisitions editor asked me to write the introductory chapter for the editorial board's review. Our literary agent said, "Never in my 20 years in the business have I seen an introductory chapter approved by an editorial board on the first submission." I exhaled.

I learned some treasured lessons from that experience. I want to share a few with you:

Nothing is arbitrary. Who calls an unqualified person to help them complete a project? People don't deliberately make stupid decisions. Whether on a job or in an industry, no one pulls your name from a hat. Either a reliable source highly recommended you, or in their search, they accumulated a substantial amount of evidence about you that led them to believe you have the ability to help complete a task. If you're like me, you've taken gradual steps to arrive at where you are today. Perhaps you aren't even aware of all that you've achieved and the skills you've built to reach your level of success.

When someone knocks on your door with a huge opportunity that you think you aren't ready for, stand on the fact that no one is going to put their job at risk for you. They're connecting with you because they believe you can make them look good.

Challenges set you up for success. Challenging experiences set you up for great opportunities. It was a long and hard journey for me to move past the mental, emotional, and physical impact of working for a boss who bullied and then fired me. She wasn't a good leader, but her insults challenged me to be a better writer. In fact, before long she was so impressed with my writing that she accused me of submitting articles and reports written by someone else.

If you've ever suffered from the fiery darts of a tyrant, then you know what a devastating effect it can have on your self-esteem. Unfortunately, your memory of negative words and behavior can remain in your psyche for years—causing you to react in ways you don't even understand.

Please stop and think about it; you learn a lot about yourself from challenging experiences. I bet, as a result, you've built or sharpened some skills you use today in your career. If you're in a situation like that today, be encouraged: Eleven years later, my former boss who fired me sent me a written apology, owning up to the issues as her own.

Mental shift. It's a mental leap. When you're standing on the ground and looking up, the sky looks vast, endless, and unreachable. From an airplane, although still amazingly massive, it appears to be within your grasp. Did the sky change, or did your position and angle change? Of course, it was your position and angle.

As you consider your next career move, it probably looks intimidating because you're thinking how different it must be to operate from that office. Instead, examine your skills, talents, abilities, and the contributions you can make to conversations that take place in that room. When you get into the boardroom with high-level players, you'll realize that they simply have the opportunity to view situations from a different angle. You have to learn their language. I'll share more about this point in the section regarding executive presence.

What you believe about yourself and your prospects of being a success are the foundation of your confidence—and the grit you possess to pursue your goals. You can claim what you believe, but your life reveals what you really think. There isn't any doubt in my mind that you're capable of becoming known for what you do and the value you add to any situation. The question is: Do you have the tools to manage your mind to navigate the challenges you'll encounter while on the path to getting there?

MIND

ELEVATION

HOW HIGH CAN YOU JUMP?

For a long time, the calculus of success has been stated as: "Eighty-five percent of success is attitude; 15% is skills and knowledge." It's now being said, "Eighty percent of success in life is showing up." Both points support the importance of mindset.

To evaluate your capacity for success, ask yourself this question: "How high can I jump?" Write down your answer. Now close your eyes, pause for a moment, and ask yourself again, "How high can I jump?" Record your response. If a specific picture came to mind or you experienced a certain feeling when you closed your eyes, include it in your response. What did you discover by completing this mind elevation exercise? Share your thoughts in your journal.

What is Mindset?

I hope you discovered, as seminar attendees typically do when I present that exercise, that when you turn inward, untapped capacity is abundant within you. So, what is mindset? It's the beliefs you hold as truths. Your opinions are shaped by the people you trust and the experiences that have significantly impacted your well-being. How you think, make decisions, and behave are predicated on what you like and dislike about yourself and others. These personal preferences also determine how people respond to you. People's regard for you directly impacts how you feel about yourself and your abilities.

When you recognize how you think and what you believe, you'll be able to identify what areas you need to develop personally to achieve what you want professionally. Smart leaders assess an organization's infrastructure before developing a strategic plan to advance its marketplace position. Likewise, it would help if you did what I call a personal appraisal of how you operate and why you function the way you do.

Why would you change how you think if you never assess the impact of what you're thinking? Do you want to develop a mindset that fosters more self-confidence? Complete the following exercise to begin evaluating and grading the strength of your current state of mind.

THE STATE OF YOUR MIND

Ask yourself the following questions to disclose your mindset. Write your answers in your journal.

1. What do I believe about my ability to achieve what I want?
2. Does my behavior align with the opinions I say I have of myself?
3. Do my daily choices reflect my beliefs?
4. What do my daily choices reveal about my ideas of myself and my abilities?
5. What evidence do I have to support the beliefs I claim I have of myself?
6. What do I believe about people?
7. How does my behavior reflect those beliefs?
8. Overall, are my beliefs and reality in alignment?
9. Am I moving in the right direction?
10. If not, what do I believe is hindering me from achieving my dreams?
11. On a scale of 1 to 10, one being least likely to get you there and ten being most likely, how would you rate your mindset?

Strategies for Change

In *Self-Esteem for Dummies*, I penned these words: "Some people thrive on change, while others struggle to understand the need to change. Stuck in the middle are those who would like to change but don't know how."

Where do you fit? Are you afraid of the unknown? Do you find it challenging to reassure yourself you'll be okay in the midst of change? From coaching hundreds of clients, I've discovered that fear is when you want a positive outcome but expect a negative one.

Since you're reading this book, I'm going to assume you're looking for answers on how to change. When change is needed, it can be hard to put what's happening into context. You can't distinguish how or where you fit, or how to navigate the nuances of change. It seems more natural to resist what's happening or to ignore it. When you do, an internal battle ensues. Your discomfort, judgment, and cynicism distort and misinterpret what's going on—making the situation excruciatingly more difficult for you to understand and tackle.

Consider the fact that you've already changed many times before, and by becoming defensive, you block opportunities for personal progress and career growth. There's no risk in doing something you've done before that didn't turn out the way you expected. Likewise, there's no risk in trying something new because you're likely to learn something you didn't know before. The greater risk is having the ball in your hands with a clear path to score, then choosing to pass the ball and someone else scores.

Keep the following in mind as lessons to embrace change and move toward mindset transformation:

Scars don't hurt. When I was three years old, my mother and I were visiting a neighbor. They had a blind dog. At the time, I was afraid of dogs. As the dog approached me, I ran. Sensing my fear, the dog ran after me and attempted to bite me in the face. My mother held up her arm to protect me. The dog bit her wrist instead. She was taken to the hospital, and a doctor closed the gash with stitches. My mother still has a faded scar on her wrist as a reminder of the lesson we both learned, but the scar doesn't hurt. Scars are reminders that you can make it through anything.

I want to make this information applicable to your challenges by differentiating between pain and a scar. When you conjure up your past feelings from some painful memory, you're pulling yourself into the pain of the past; this behavior blurs the lines of truth, and you fail to see the facts.

When you can look back on a situation without emotion, you're able to see that it's a fading scar and you're able to process the current challenge better. For example, my mother being bitten by the dog didn't intensify my fear of dogs. Instead, my parents gave me the information I needed to interact with dogs more successfully, and the incident helped me better manage my fears.

Be still until you're ready. Once you accept the need to change, you owe it to yourself to find your center of gravity and take time to plan your transition. People will talk. They'll tell you what you should and should not do based on what they would do. Don't cave into the pressure to make quick decisions based on what's right for them. Instead, focus on what's right for you. Accurately read the landscape, be still, figure out how you want to play, then make your move.

Write a statement of stance. You've been through challenges before, and you made it to the other side. That's because you're agile and have what you need within you to take a stance against procrastination, fears of inferiority, and other negative thoughts about yourself. When you reflect on a time when you adapted and changed, you remind yourself of how incredibly bold and powerful you are. Challenge yourself, and you'll elevate yourself.

MIND

ELEVATION

STATEMENT OF CONVICTION

Write a statement of conviction you want to live by that elevates your thinking and inspires you to act. I've provided questions to get you thinking. Read it daily because repetition fuels action.

1. Think about a time when you had to change. Why did you need to change?
2. What did you need to change?
3. How did you feel when you realized you needed to change?
4. How did you feel after the change?
5. What steps did you take to embrace change?
6. Write a statement about your ability to change and the value you get from changing.

Overcome Moments of Uncertainty

During an interview, I was asked this question:

> What has been the hardest part about walking your talk where it required more effort, more discipline, more concentration, and more overcoming negative beliefs for you to be fully S. Renee?

Switch my name for yours, and think about how you would answer that question. We all have moments of internal conflict. During these times, our thoughts get twisted, and we question ourselves and our ability to prosper. Anguish, worry, doubt, and stress are signs that a mindset of lack and limitation are affecting you more than your belief that you can accomplish what you want.

So how do you get beyond moments of doubt that rob you of your confidence? You don't. You thank and embrace these moments of insecurity for showing up because they're trying to get your attention. They're telling you that something has to change.

The purpose of uncertainty is to awaken you and disrupt your need to meet the expectations of others. Think about a time when you felt uncertain. What were you thinking? What questions challenged you? I suspect you remember asking yourself, "Am I saying the right thing? Will they like my presentation? Is this how they want me to do this?"

When your thoughts are focused on what you think other people expect of you, that's you trying to adhere to someone else's methods. The reality is those are your thoughts, your expectations—and your dysfunction. You can interrupt moments that make you question yourself; the mere fact that you're aware of such moments helps you to take your power back.

Here's my answer to the interviewer's question mentioned above. Due to its length, I'm paraphrasing:

I'm still evolving into S. Renee. I'm still getting to know, love, and accept her. I don't think I'm there, and I suspect I won't get there anytime soon. I'm on a journey just like you—imperfect in some areas of my life and a master of others. As a speaker and writer, there was a time when I questioned whether people would like me. I had to find my space, my uniqueness, and my own voice, and trust that when I had a presentation, I could deliver it with the passion and power needed to make a difference in people's lives. That was a demon I've fought for years.

MIND

ELEVATION

BREAK THE CYCLE

In your journal, draw a horizontal line down the middle of the page to create two columns. Label the columns: I Feel Uncertain When, and The Truth Is. Think about personal and professional conversations you've had with others that made you feel uncertain. You likely had an uneasy feeling in your body or critical thoughts of yourself.

In the first column, outline the details of the situation. Include when you questioned yourself, why, and with whom. In the second column, write the truth of what was happening, based on your observation of the situation. Note what you discover about yourself, the conditions under which you become uncertain, and with whom.

Are the Risks Too High or Is Your Confidence Too Low?

How do you feel about yourself compared to how you want to feel about yourself? Are you where you want to be? Do you consider the risks too high to pursue what you want? Have you considered that your confidence may be too low?

Taking each step through this process helps you navigate challenges you think threaten your opportunities for advancement and value to an organization. It also enables you to identify your relevance to the evolving workplace while clarifying the role you want to play in it.

When you do your internal work and establish a plan for how you'll get what you want, you give yourself a reason to be attentive to your brand. Incorporate the next four steps into your life to embrace change and move toward mindset transformation:

Step 1: Know where you want to go. Do you feel as though you're in a rut and can't get out? If so, you're not alone. That's a common description of how a person feels when they are in transition. What's interesting about that is many people I talk to have a hard time communicating what they want. By traveling from one place to another, you've learned that you have to know where you're going to get there. Your fundamental decisions about your life and career are the foundation of your brand. Deciding what you want makes finding the path easier and getting there faster.

DECIDE WHAT YOU WANT

At the top of your page, write My Dreams. Set a timer for two minutes. Without any reservations, write down what you want. Don't limit yourself. When the alarm rings, stop. Review your responses. Keep your answers near; you'll revisit them later.

Step 2: Pinpoint where you are. Pinpointing your location is an essential step to transformation, especially if you're in the middle of brand and mindset evaluations. When you identify how you think and what you believe, you'll isolate the areas of your thinking and behavior that need further development.

How far are you from where you want to be? Do you know if you're facing the right direction? To choose your next step, you have to recognize the value of your work and the magnitude of the lessons you've learned along the way—the information you compile channels your thinking toward the first step to brand development.

IDENTIFY WHAT YOU HAVE

Refer to your dream list. At the top of a new page, transfer your first desire listed. Based on that ambition, complete the following statements. Record your responses.

1. I can achieve this goal because I am_____.
2. The positions I've held that validate my credentials to achieve this goal are_____.
3. The lessons I've learned that will help me achieve my desire are_____.
4. The relevant skills, talents, and abilities I've developed that will help me reach my goal are_____.

Step 3: Assess your human connections. Networks are your lifeline to success. The more successful your personal and professional networks—and your access network—the more successful you can become. Let me explain access network. An access network is a group of people you don't have a direct connection to, but you have access to them through someone you know personally. For example, when I was looking for a corporate sponsor for an event I was planning, I didn't know any corporate sponsorship decision-makers. However, I knew a banking executive. She didn't make decisions on corporate sponsorship, but she knew who did. I reached out to her, and she scheduled a meeting with the bank's corporate sponsorship decision maker, herself, and me. The bank became a sponsor.

For this reason, it's paramount that you know who's in your network and how they perceive you. Do you know who you can rely on for help when you need it? Who are the people impressed with you and your work to the degree they'd endorse you? You have to have a group of influencers in your corner who you can call when you need assistance. Knowing who they are before you need them is imperative. I share more on this subject in the step, Position Your Brand and Practice Executive Presence.

MIND

ELEVATION

INVENTORY YOUR NETWORK

Make a list of everyone you know in a position of power who will vouch for you. Then make a list of the people you would like to be in your network. If someone in your current network can introduce you to someone you'd like to meet, list them together.

Step 4: Commit to being flexible. Success is a direct result of being accountable for your life and choices. You have power over who you want to be, where you want to go, and how you get there. At any time, you can go in a different direction. Whatever you choose as your life's mission, persist until you get to where you want to be. Always hold onto to the thought that your happiness and freedom to be authentically you come first. Also, keep in mind that as you grow and discover more about yourself and what you enjoy doing, you can change or adjust accordingly. Several important points to keep in mind:

You are never the victim. The commitment isn't to the process or to become a national expert. The promise is taking ownership of yourself and your life so that you can become whoever and whatever you want to be.

You have to be a reliable resource. Elevating your career opportunities requires you to commit to obtaining and sharing a body of knowledge and providing a service that adds value to the people who need it.

Brand development is an intentional process. Brand development is the process through which you identify who you are and who you need to be to connect with your audience so they'll listen to you. I'm not proposing you manipulate or dishonor who you are. I'm trusting you have the integrity to be yourself as you take this journey of assessing who you are at your core.

IDENTIFY WHAT YOU'RE MISSING

Review your notes to refresh your mind about where you are in the process. Complete the following statement:

To expand my capacity for success, I need_____.

Step 5: Elevate Your Mind to Match Your Mark. You're an astute professional. Even so, you're finding it difficult to move beyond the hurts of the past. Maybe your parents didn't raise you, your husband left you, or the beautiful girl from high school married your best friend.

Unpleasant circumstances happen in all our lives. Unfortunately, for many people, they become pain points that manifest themselves later in many forms. You've probably seen them in the workplace bully, the arrogant boss, or the backstabbing co-worker. You may have felt them yourself when blaming politics for being overlooked for a promotion, becoming defensive during a performance review, or overselling yourself after a potential client just said, "You have a deal." It's the pain versus faded-scar syndrome I mentioned earlier.

I had a client named Jessica, one of my smartest clients. She came to me after years of failed therapy. She believed she needed to redesign her brand. She was a director at a company and was torn between entrepreneurship and applying for an executive director's role at the organization where she worked. By our third session, it was clear to me that her emotional turbulence had nothing to do with the organization or her desire to venture out on her own. She was stuck in the past, rooted in negative thoughts and feelings about herself and how she was raised. She gave every excuse to explain why she couldn't move beyond it.

You have to believe that if you want success, you can have it. However, you have to be willing to do the work to achieve the success you want. Your mindset has to be in alignment with what you want. Whenever you choose to step back instead of stepping up, you communicate uncertainty to yourself and others. When you're unsure about your abilities, what you say and do reflects your opinion of yourself. One of my favorite quotes is from Dr. Michael Bernard Beckwith, "You can't hide your secret thoughts because they show up as your life." If you don't trust yourself, why should anyone else believe in you?

It's imperative that you deal with your internal challenges before redesigning your brand. For my clients, it's a prerequisite.

Jessica and I spent over three months working together. In the end, she told me, "You are the most challenging and compassionate person I have worked with thus far." From my perspective, the needle hadn't moved far, and I had to accept that she just wasn't ready.

I don't want you to set yourself up to fail by falling short because of some unresolved emotional block. If you need deeper self-exploration for mindset evaluation, I like authors Eckhart Tolle and Lisa Nichols. Lisa Nichols endorsed my first book, *There Is More Inside: Personal Essentials Needed for Living a Power-Packed Life*. In it, I share my life stories and mental breakthroughs while helping readers achieve theirs. You can also visit my YouTube channel (youtube.com/user/sreneesmith) to view hundreds of self-development videos. Most importantly, find an author or expert who speaks to you.

A Mindset for Success

You may have been told that if you visualize, affirm, and fearlessly work toward what you want, you'll get it. In my opinion, there are several requirements absent from this model: a workable plan, a personal brand that sets you apart and gets you noticed, and the people you need to coach, mentor, and sponsor you.

As you've learned, your mindset is the cornerstone to building and sustaining a bankable brand. Here's a list of specific actions you can take to build the right mindset:

1. **Find a truth you can believe in.** What you believe about yourself and others should be an asset in your life. Everything you think isn't the truth, and every thought doesn't deserve to be spoken. Objectively ask yourself: Is this the truth? If not, what is? If you patiently wait for the answer, you'll instinctually know what you should and shouldn't say. Challenge your beliefs. Be open to new revelations, and apply new solutions to your life.

2. **Live ideas that nurture and support you.** More than anyone else, you need you. You need to love, believe, and support yourself and your dreams. Dump whatever behavior doesn't make you feel good about being you. Although not easy, it's not complicated. It's a decision to love, honor, and be kind to yourself.

3. **Honor yourself and others.** You're important, and everyone is equally significant. Honor others by giving them space to have their ideas, opinions, and ways of getting things done, and show yourself the same respect.

4. **Let integrity be your guide.** Challenges will come, unexpected situations will occur, and you'll have to make tough decisions. Before giving your final answer, check in with yourself to ensure you're in alignment with integrity.

5. **Live your passion.** Waking up every day to do what you enjoy is a dimension of personal and professional fulfillment that you and everyone around you deserve to experience. If you are miserable, stop, take time to find out why, and change directions. Look for prospects that interest you, and, regardless of whether you think you're qualified or not, put your name in the hat. That's the only way you'll know if it's the opportunity for you.

6. **Ask for what you need.** Asking for help can make you feel vulnerable. Not letting people know what you need or want can disempower or limit you. If you present yourself well and have a decent brand, you'll discover that many people will gladly assist you.

7. **Believe something more significant is at work.** There will be times when things won't go as planned. Whatever happens, believe it's in the best interest of you and everyone involved. Learn the lesson and keep pressing forward.

MIND

ELEVATION

TRANSFORMATION FOR YOUR TRANSITION

Reflect on what would enable you to attain greater personal and professional fulfillment. Add your favorites to the list discussed above. Pen them in your journal.

CHAPTER 2
YOUR BRAND

IN THIS CHAPTER I define personal brand and describe the brand development process. I give you the tools to assess the strengths of your current brand and identify areas of your brand identity that need your attention. Chances are high you already know your flaws. Perhaps you didn't know the advantages of changing until now, or you didn't know what you needed to do to improve the results you're getting. Knowing that everyone has an agenda and that you should have one, too, will help you see greater possibilities for your personal and professional relationships.

Depending on where you are, personal brand development can be a lengthy, complex, and challenging process. However, it's a must-have, and I'm going to simplify its significance by giving you the two questions everyone silently asks themselves when they meet you. By the end of this chapter, you'll appreciate the power of your brand and gain the motivation to redesign it.

Why Branding?

Branding is the result of the need people and businesses have to be heard in a loud, competitive marketplace where everyone is screaming for attention. As you think about television and online advertisements, social media updates, and digital billboards, you realize companies are creatively working to distinguish themselves so that you'll pay attention to them. Do you ever think critically about the difficulty you've experienced in getting the attention of your audience? If you don't know who your audiences are and what these potential clients or customers need, why do you want their attention? What would you do with it? Why should they be responsive to you if you don't care about them? A big challenge I discovered for many people is identifying their audience, crafting a message they'd respond to, and sharing pertinent information with them.

Sophia, a senior leader, at a retail organization contacted me about branding for her new book. She was struggling to get the attention she wanted. Throughout our conversation, she'd make glaring and disturbing self-deprecating remarks. I brought this to her attention by using an example of a group of senior female leaders I had worked with at a Fortune 500 corporation.

I shared with her that one of the women found the self-discovery process so difficult that she started crying when she struggled to list three adjectives to describe herself. According to her, she was raised in an Italian family in Tennessee, and she was taught that women weren't supposed to talk about themselves. These are the types of internal issues some women face that hinder them from effectively communicating their competence and showcasing their abilities to senior leaders.

I shared with Sophia how negative statements about herself minimize her power and shifts people's perception of her. Whether sincere or used as a weapon tomanipulate people, self-critical remarks look more like emotional maneuvering and power shifting than genuine low self-esteem. For whatever reason it is done, I advise against it.

I've worked with corporations that have more than 30,000 workers. With a talent pool this deep, how you differentiate yourself from other smart, amazing colleagues determines who listens to you. I developed this illustration when I first started teaching branding. I still use it to explain to audiences the reason for brands.

It starts with the awareness that human behaviors cause problems. Everyone has at least one problem. The dilemma could be health complications, workplace issues, dysfunctional family relationships, conflict in government, or broken education and healthcare systems. Problems create needs. People are looking for answers to

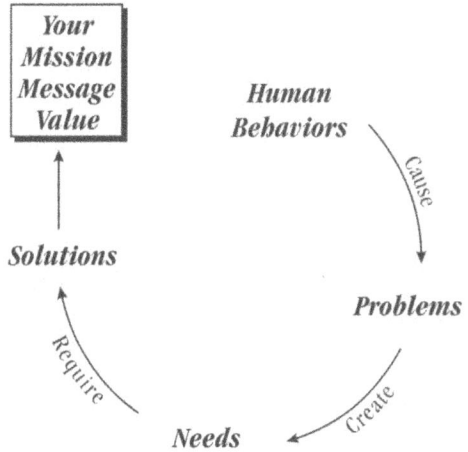

questions that they ponder, agonize over, and worry about every day. These may be situations that rock them at their core, disturb their family's well-being, and deprive them of any stabilizing peace. What you offer is the solution to their problem. Your brand communicates your mission, message, and value. When done intentionally, it's easier for people to find you.

IDENTIFY THE PROBLEM

Think about the problems employees and leaders at your workplace deal with daily. Challenges such as:

- Managing costs to yield a profit
- Developing practical products to expand market share
- Creating an effective marketing plan for a new product launch
- Writing persuasive reports

- Streamlining processes
- Inspiring peak performance

List additional challenges you see people struggling with and add them to the list. Next, focus on what you want to do by writing a list of major problems you see or hear about in your company or generally in the world around you. Answer these questions:

1. Who has the problem?
2. How is the challenge impacting the person personally and professionally?
3. How is the issue affecting the organization?
4. How is the situation being dealt with currently?

The Power of Branding

The reason you haven't reached the success you want isn't that you aren't smart enough or don't have the ability. If you reflect on why you haven't achieved a goal, you'll probably discover that, like most people, you started with hope, thirst, and focus. When you faced a complex task or when your audience didn't respond to you immediately, you abandoned your goal and settled for an opportunity less challenging to accomplish. Changing your mind meant going in a different direction, losing momentum, and your marketplace position.

This approach to life has led you to where you are today. It's highly probable you were expecting to be farther along in your life and career. Still, this isn't entirely your fault. You've been trained to believe that developing goals, objectives, and action steps would keep you motivated. However, for many people, goals don't give you satisfaction even after reaching them.

Instead, knowing why you want something provides the drive you need to keep pressing forward when you'd otherwise give up. I'm not diminishing the importance of goals; in fact, I'm adding value to setting goals. Think of it this way: There's a difference between setting goals and knowing what you want to happen and why you want it to happen.

Goals provide a focal point and determine what actions you should take. When you know what you want to happen and why, the answers illuminate the significance of the goal. I've witnessed clients who developed goals go from exhausted and frustrated to enthused and cheerful. With greater clarity comes an energy shift and a surge of creativity and momentum.

Luke is a real estate agent and entrepreneur with a patent pending for boxing gloves. He attended my one-day workshop on branding because he needed to raise money for his invention. In approximately ten days after the seminar, he followed up with me to share that he had raised double the amount he needed in seven days. He said, "S. Renee opened my mind to what was possible and helped remove the barriers I thought I had." The truth is that I gave him tools and strategies, and he used them.

Here are additional thoughts on the power of a brand:

- It communicates your value and sets you apart from others.
- It demands the attention of your audiences and fuels their interest in wanting to know more about you.
- It positions you as a subject-matter expert.
- It boosts your confidence in yourself and your product or service.
- It promotes what you do and opens the door to new opportunities and endless possibilities.

MIND

ELEVATION

THE POWER OF YOUR BRAND

Make a list of what you want your brand to create for you.

What People Want to Know About You

You've heard of Oprah Winfrey. You've seen the golden arches, and it's likely you've worn the swoosh image of Nike. Names, faces, and symbols all mean something, but what? The "what" identifies the brand and communicates its anticipated value.

As you evaluate your brand, see if it connects with your audience. Does it fulfill its promise, and do your income, influence, and opportunities reflect what you do, how you do it, and the value you bring to the lives of others? Management, customers, family, and friends are watching you. They're observing how you react in various situations. Observers want to understand what you want, how you operate, and what you do to get what you want. When people meet or interact with you, they're silently asking themselves two questions:

1. What are you worth to me?
2. How much are you going to cost me?

No one engages with your brand without an interest in what you have to offer. It's the need of your audience that draws them to you. Once you have their attention, they are evaluating the legitimacy of your brand. The question "What are you worth to me?" is a probe into your competence. "How much are you going to cost me?" is an examination of your trustworthiness. A leader once said this about an employee:

"I wish I could buy him for what he's worth and sell him for what he thinks he's worth."

The attention your audience gives you is a clue that you're offering something they need, and your brand speaks to them. The experience you create for them when interacting with you is what solidifies their perception of you. It's the experience that makes them want to further engage with you and ultimately pay for your services. Have you ever known a person who would tell you how wonderful you are but wouldn't respond to your emails or phone calls? When you finally spoke with them, they'd give you an excuse about why they didn't respond to you. It's simple: Behaviors don't lie; people do. An extra five seconds to click reply and type "on the go...will follow up shortly" would leave you with a different feeling, wouldn't it?

That's why it's paramount that you know your message and how your audience is interpreting it. When people evaluate what it will cost them to interact with you, they're not just thinking of financial costs. They want to know how they'll benefit from the exchange—or suffer if they invite you into their personal space and professional network.

Everyone is looking for good things to come to them—including you. Are you clear about what you bring to the table? When you build your brand correctly, here's the outcome: People recognize you and know what they can expect from you.

HOW MUCH DO YOU CHARGE?

What are you charging people to interact with you? Do you cost them time, money, productivity, or relationships? Consider the questions below. Think analytically about yourself and the effect your decisions have on the lives of others. Answer the following items from the other person's viewpoint:

1. What do I get as a result of interacting with you?
2. How do I feel after conversing with you?
3. Would I like to communicate with you again?

What is Personal Branding?

Allison, an award-winning senior executive at a telecommunications company, called me after a 30-year career because she wanted to rebrand herself. As she put it, "I want to be the S. Renee of my industry." She revealed to me her desire to share what she'd learned over the years about how people's behavior impacts their careers, and I was amazed to hear her confidently affirm, "I don't want this to be about me. I don't want to brand myself; I want to brand what I do."

I responded, "Branding isn't about you. It's about the people you serve. Branding is about how you package, position, and promote yourself. The way you craft and communicate who you are and the value you bring to the lives of others play a major role in who finds and connects with you. Branding is about the value you bring to others." She replied, "Oh, I like the way you said that."

Allison's perception of personal branding is a common misconception. Personal brand development is the deliberate process to package you, position what you do, and promote the results you create. Your audience can be leadership, a potential client, or co-workers—maybe all three. Depending on what you want to achieve, your audience can be a community, a congregation, or any person or group of people you want to assist in resolving a specific problem.

My branding development model is one of self-actualization. I developed it that way because your brand is an extension of who you are at your core. It's not a separate, fictitious entity that comes to your rescue when you've committed a faux pas. When you package who you are authentically and promote what you do truthfully, you build a sustainable, credible brand.

I had a client named David. He worked at a university as executive director of student retention. Despite exceeding retention goals and obtaining scholarly success, he was having a difficult time landing a promotion. As we began to devise a plan for his advancement, I asked the following questions: What is your ultimate goal? Why do you believe you're being overlooked? Could there be some unknown concerns about your performance, personality, or persona that leadership may not be telling you? What is the culture of the organization? Do you have on-campus partnerships and alliances? With whom?

Without all the answers to these questions, we started the process by defining his brand based on his perception. He viewed himself as knowledgeable, hardworking, and results-oriented. I then encouraged David to ask his team, leadership, and some colleagues how they would describe his brand.

We discovered that his staff and co-workers also viewed him as very knowledgeable, hardworking, and results-oriented. Management thought he was a good partner but a micromanager who spent too much time performing tasks that should be delegated. University officials said they were looking for a visionary leader, someone who develops staff and encourages creative conversations to find solutions.

Here's what the president shared with me during a lunch meeting that no one had told David:

> Under my leadership, David will never get a promotion. He's an awful leader who doesn't know how to talk to people. His staff comes to my office all the time with complaints about him.

I couldn't believe what I was hearing. David didn't know about that feedback. Perhaps he didn't ask the right people, or nobody dared to tell him the truth. I know this for sure: If the president felt that strongly about him, I'm confident there was a buzz about it on campus.

Do you ever wonder why you can't get to the next level in your career? Perhaps you get excellent performance reviews, ace projects, and do what you're told to do. You even stay late and sacrifice vacation days to get the job done. Based on the facts, how does leadership view you? Are you an innovative partner who they're watching for future advancement? Alternatively, are you the employee that's dedicated to the company but doesn't understand how to position your intellectual property to help foster your growth?

A personal brand represents the conclusion people draw about who you are, what you do, and how you operate that impacts them. It's the feeling and image they get when they think of you. Your brand answers the internal question, "Can you make my life better? If so, how?"

Think of your brand in terms of a product. Every product is positioned to promise you money, power, love, or sex. Personal brands do the same thing. For instance, I help my clients increase their income and influence by becoming more likable, marketable, and credible.

Depending on the mentality of the person I'm working with, they may think the combination of money and influence will also yield love and sex. Personal brands also satisfy those same needs. For example, you're a sales manager. Your team is responsible for increasing profits through higher sales. As frontline employees, you build a relationship with customers. Your role directly affects profits, marketplace presence, and reputation management. Think of the organization as your customer. Your performance increases its profits, power, and marketplace position.

Bring the impact of your brand closer to your customer, the vice president of sales. She's your actual customer because your performance directly impacts her and how leadership perceives her brand. I want to clarify a misconception. During media interviews, some hosts introduce me and say, "Branding is another word for reputation." I don't subscribe to the philosophy that branding and reputation are the same. Reputation is your character, which comprises your personality and your moral compass. Reputation governs how you go about getting things done. The brand has a broader agenda. It includes your reputation and every aspect of who you are, including the problems you solve. I discuss this in more detail in Part Two.

Are you deliberate in the way you present yourself? Are you mindful of what you say and how you say it? Do you discern how you make people feel? Do you know the image your audiences have of you?

Have you ever noticed that when a person goes to court for an alleged crime they've committed, their lawyers strategically plan how the defendant should present themselves? The reason is simple: They want to control the judge and the jury's perception and sway their decision in the defendant's favor.

How attentive the defendant is to the legal team's advice plays a role in the outcome of the case. You have tremendous control over how people view you and the result of your interactions. As in a court case, people assess two parts of your brand:

1. Clues about who you are, based on what you're presenting
2. Your track record, which tells them who you've been

Don't even think about abusing the power of branding. The point of branding isn't to create an image for people to follow. Branding is about creating an appetite for the purpose you're on earth to serve.

Regardless of people's perception of you right now, by redesigning your brand, you can get people talking positively about you. In Part Two of this book, I cover how to package, position, and promote yourself. For now, accept that you have a brand and the power to change it.

MIND

ELEVATION

IMAGINE

Close your eyes and imagine for a moment you wake up every day knowing what you have to do, whose lives you touch, and the impact you make on those lives. As you work on projects you're passionate about, people are chattering about how phenomenal you are and the assistance you provide in helping them achieve their goals. You receive unexpected calls from people seeking to compensate you for your services. As the go-to person in your industry, you enjoy your life thoroughly. That's the power of having a compelling personal brand!

Evaluate Your Brand

Monique, an introvert, hadn't had a promotion in six years. She heard me speak at an event and a few months later signed up for one of my workshops. Monique then purchased one of my group coaching packages. A program assistant at the time of our meeting, she landed two job interviews within four months after becoming my client. She received offers for both positions and decided to accept an assistant director's position.

Shortly after that, she was promoted to director. Within 15 months of redesigning her brand, her income increased 113 percent, and she was named Employee of the Year. Did the culture of her former workplace fail to measure employee engagement and job satisfaction? Possibly; that's not uncommon. Did management overlook Monique's potential? That's highly probable. Studies confirm that within organizations, internal talent often goes undiscovered. Nonetheless, We couldn't control what leadership did or didn't do. What we could control, we did. We started by evaluating Monique's brand.

Through the process, she determined she wasn't representing her skills, talents, abilities, and experiences at her current level of her performance. Monique was having a difficult time visualizing herself at the level of success I knew she was capable of achieving. She says, "S. Renee sees the invisible in people." I believe that, on an unconscious level, she knew everything I was seeing was there, but it was difficult for her to comprehend and communicate the immense value of her skills to an organization.

It's tough to see what others see in you when you haven't assessed what you have to offer. Once Monique took inventory of what she had to offer, she knew what she had, why she had it, what she could do with it, and the value of her expertise. At that point, there was a mindset shift. We were able to transform her brand, and she transcended her goals.

MIND

ELEVATION

EXAMINE YOUR BRAND

Fill in the blanks and document your responses.

1. My audiences are_____.
2. My audiences rely on me for_____.
3. My audiences describe me as_____.
4. My audiences thank me for_____.
5. I promise my audiences I can_____.
6. If my audiences didn't get help from me, they would call _____.
7. If my audiences didn't get help, it would cost them _____.

Untapped Talent

Early in my speaking career, international motivational speaker and author Les Brown said, "S. Renee, you don't know what you don't know and don't even realize you don't know it." Failing to notice you don't know something is dangerous. On the other hand, it's tragic if you recognize you need more knowledge and you ignore the urgency to get it. Being aware that your life and career aren't going in the direction that you want, and unaware of what's hindering you, confirm your need to evaluate your brand.

The purpose of brand evaluation is to uncover what's working for you and what's working against you. When you pay attention to how your behavior is shaping a person's experience with you, you'll have more influence over the opportunities that come your way.

Here's what you need to know:

Communicate your power. People who you want to hire, follow, or love you, are looking for more than a good person. They're looking for the right partner. Partners are people who are effective communicators. They collaborate with others, make thoughtful, critical decisions, and seek opportunities for continuous learning. They're ambitious and tenacious problem solvers who are accountable for their choices. They aren't waiting for permission to drive positive change; they take calculated risks that advance the partnership.

If you bring your A-game to the fight every day, and your brand communicates up front that you help your audiences meet objectives, then you're the right partner. If you present yourself as a nice person who does an average to good job but prefers things remain the same, then you need to rethink your brand.

I was having a fact-finding session with a potential client. He's a sales manager at a healthcare company, who was explaining some challenges the company was having with meeting sales projections. I inquired about the company's brand. He mentioned that, despite having a long history and excellent relationships with doctors and their teams, these individuals say they consider his company "nice and a good partner." However, they often choose the company's competitors, who are assertive newcomers.

Never confuse being friendly with loyalty or longevity with faithfulness. Your brand has to evolve and change with the needs of your audience and the market. Like clients, forward-thinking leaders are shifting company cultures and projecting how to attract, recruit, and retain the most dynamic trailblazers. Leaders, clients, and companions want to feel certain that when you agree to take on a project it will be finished on time, carried out with excellence, and considered complete at the end of the conversation with you. To be clear, they don't want to have to worry about it after it's been put in your hands.

Confidence in you starts with your presentation style. In Part Two, I go into detail about your brand package and how to develop executive presence. For the moment, let's discuss the impact of how you present yourself.

What does your presentation style say about you? Monique was able to obtain extraordinary success so quickly because she didn't make excuses or deny the need for leadership to know, like, and trust her. She took ownership of the flaws in her brand and why they gave her audience a false negative reading.

She acknowledged that she could have engaged with leadership more to ensure they knew the impact of her work. Besides, she could have stated her career goals so that management understood she was looking for career growth opportunities. The nonverbal messages she sent were contrary to who she is and what she wanted. She enjoyed working with her colleagues. She wanted leadership to notice her, appreciate her curiosity, and recognize her quest for advancement.

Monique kept her distance because she didn't want to appear to be overstepping her manager or buttering up to senior leaders. Plus, she assumed they knew about her admirable qualities. Why wouldn't they? Every day she arrived early and stayed late. She was intelligent, hardworking, willing to take on additional responsibilities, and the customers loved her. Annual performance reviews confirmed her superior decision-making skills and her ability to partner. Still, years passed without a single mention of a promotion. She had reached her breaking point. It was time to go.

Before her first interview, we discussed how to use verbal and nonverbal communication to demonstrate poise and inspire enthusiasm for what she would bring to the position. We crafted questions to ask the interviewer to display her curiosity. We reviewed how to use pauses and make friends with silence. She learned when to sit back in her chair to suggest maturity and thoughtfulness and how to lean forward to express attentiveness and interest. What she said, wore, and how she presented herself proved to be spot-on because it all worked in her favor.

Do you want to activate in your life what Monique did to advance her career? Then do what she did and start by evaluating your brand.

MIND

ELEVATION

PERCEPTIONS MATTER

Write down three adjectives you think describe you. Then ask at least three people to provide you with three attributes they would use to represent you. Select a diverse group of people, for example, a family member, a co-worker, and a customer. Consider a pastor, neighbor, and friend.

Give everyone permission to be honest with you by reassuring them you're open to their feedback. Most importantly, regardless of what they say or don't say, never debate, defend or force them to justify their opinions. Once you receive all responses, record and review them. Compare them to see which words repeat. The most consistent words represent your brand.

PART TWO

PERSONAL BRAND AND EXECUTIVE PRESENCE DEVELOPMENT

It was pouring down rain, and I was driving from the home office of the company I worked for to the client's office. I was going to drop off a demo copier to a customer who I had not met. As I made the turn onto the driveway leading up to the company's home office, I was terrified by what I saw. Steps! How the heck was I going to get the gurney with a heavy, oversize copier on it, through the mud, up to the steps, and into their office—in a suit and high heels.

I jumped out of the car and immediately felt the cold rain soak my hair and pour down my face. I ran to the back of the station wagon, opened the tailgate, and grabbed the handle of the gurney. I pulled; it budged slightly. I pulled again; it moved a bit closer to the back end of the car. I yanked as hard as I could, and BANG! The copier fell off the gurney. The harsh sound of heavy, hard plastic hitting the cement was terrorizing. "Is it broken?" I wondered. Already drenched, I struggled to get the copier back on the gurney and into the car.

Exhausted, I ran back up to the door and rang the bell. The customer opened the door and greeted me:

"Poor thing. Please come in."

"No, thank you," I said. "I'm too wet and muddy. I just wanted to let you know that I was here and need to reschedule. The copier fell out of the car, and I need to bring you another one."

Seemingly not hearing what I said, she responded, "Are you sure you don't want to come in?"

Embarrassed, I formed a fake smile. "No," I said. "I'll call you."

I wasn't fond of the job before, but now I hated it. That day I decided I wasn't going to delay any longer pursuing my teenage dream of becoming a model. During the exit interview, the sales manager asked me why I was leaving. I told him I was going to become a model. He laughed and said, "You'll never make money as a model. There are great opportunities for you here." I didn't respond. It was apparent he couldn't see beyond my conservative blue suit and white shirt.

Are you craving your next career move? In Part One, you evaluated your mindset, decided what you wanted and who you wanted to be, and assessed your brand. Some of the information and responses were probably a confirmation of what you already knew, but you may have also discovered new things about yourself that sparked fresh ideas and thoughts worthy of reflection.

In this section, I share the strategy I used to repackage, position, and promote myself so that I could transition from corporate employee to entertainment personality, then through academia and management positions to nationally recognized self-development guru.

Like my clients, I bet you want a likable package you'd be proud to promote, that produces an eagerness in others to engage with you. This section aids in the design of that package. As you go through the process, your idea of who you want to be may shift, or you may choose to serve a different audience. You might even discover that you want to do something entirely different. Regardless of what you decide, follow the content mindfully to build a bankable brand and executive presence that will make you more likable, marketable, and credible—elevating your visibility while enhancing your career.

STEP 1

PACKAGE YOUR BRAND AND DEVELOP EXECUTIVE PRESENCE

YOU HAVE IT ALL—education, a proven track record of success, and industry recognition. Still, something is missing. Here's what a client, a senior leader in the educational field, says happened to him when he went through this process:

> Our sessions started in one direction, but midway through they became my personal journey of affirmation and self-discovery. S. Renee asks the right questions and provides precise feedback that leaves the customer with no excuses [but to go] toward self-fulfillment. Buckle your seat belts, ladies and gentlemen. Even if you are a skeptic, I found that a real career coach grows your belief in yourself and gives you the tools to change your world by answering those lifelong, nagging questions, "What do I want to be when I grow up?" and "How do I get there?"

Are you a big fish in a pond? Are you a little fish in the ocean? Have you outgrown your brand or does it need more muscle? Regardless, you need a brand package that piques others' interest in you. What do people do to catch your attention? Is it their presence? How do they dress? Is it the way they walk, talk, or interact with other people?

If you want to advance to expert status or if you are an expert and want people to notice your intellectual property and innovative ideas, you have to know what's going to get you there. Your brand package is what entices your audience and invites them to engage with you.

In this chapter, you'll create your brand package and develop the executive presence you need to woo your audience and have them coming back for more of what you have to offer them.

Your Brand Package Components

Starting with your brand package helps to sharpen your vision of who you are, the value you bring to your audience, and the impression you want to leave with them. Your brand package includes the following components:

1. Your Vision Statement
2. Your Mission Statement
3. Your Message
4. Your Value
5. Your Personality, Persona, and Presence
6. Your Presentation Style
7. Your Likability Factor

What You Need to Know

Before you start redesigning your brand to become more likable, marketable, and credible, keep these five critical points in mind:

1. **Know the terms and conditions.** Do your homework and count up the costs to pursue your goals. When your aim is high, it takes extraordinary skills, willpower, resources, and relationships to hit the target. Know what you need to qualify for the position or opportunity you're seeking.

2. **Understand the value of your brand.** Your brand is your calling card. As you build it, make sure it's who you want to be and how you want to represent yourself. As you go through each exercise and respond to each question or statement, be true to yourself.

3. **Be open and objective.** Be open to internal prompts that will dare you to say the things about yourself you've always wanted to say but didn't have the courage or confidence to speak. Seeing yourself as a brand opens up greater possibilities for you as you go through the process.

4. **Have fun.** Creating your brand is a fun journey of discovering how incredibly exceptional and amazing you are. Your thoughts will wander, and your dreams will take you on great adventures. Go with them and find the love, laughter, and life you deserve.

5. **Trust the branding process.** Brands create success. You'll package, position, and promote your brand. It will take you a fair distance, and then you'll have to repackage your brand based on your growth and new goals. Be consistent in your behavior and flexible in your thinking. Adjustments will always be necessary.

Understanding the Brand Development Process

The process starts with questions. The answers help you develop your brand, which includes assessing your value. I created the illustration (next page) to show the course of the brand development process. Start at the lower left-hand box (in the first column), which asks, "Why are you here?" Your answer helps you identify your mission. Since your mission provides a solution to a problem, that's what makes you likable. Still in the bottom row, move to the second-column question, "Where are you a gateway to?" Wherever you lead your audience, they will reap benefits from you, which make you marketable. The third column of the bottom row asks, "What results do you create?" Your consistent outcomes increase your credibility.

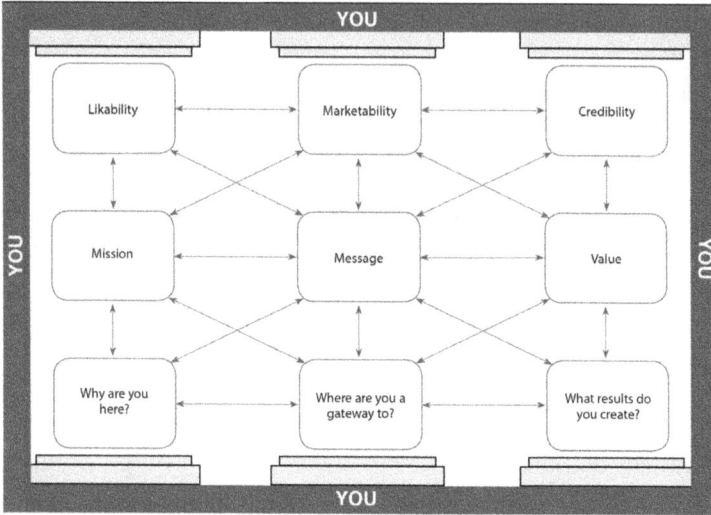

Your Vision Statement

As a little girl, I'd pretend I was in an interview with the press. I recall playing both the interviewer and interviewee. I'd ask myself questions about my success, then answer them out loud. In my case, life imitates play, and today the media requests my expertise on topics that impact people's personal and professional lives.

Most children are imaginative and have a great vision for themselves before it gets suppressed by unqualified family members, friends, teachers, athletic coaches, and bosses. The image you once held as your future may still linger inside you. Perhaps over the years another secret dream has emerged.

Your vision statement serves as your guiding light. Every decision you make should move you closer to who you want to be, what you want to do, and how you want to express yourself in the world. Without a vision statement, you don't know if you're on your desired path.

Why You Need a Vision Statement

Do you feel overworked? Are you often fatigued and frustrated? Do you abandon your goals to help others reach theirs? In the October 22, 2018, issue of *Woman's World*, the column "Ask America's Ultimate Experts" gave readers tips about how to say no. Here's what the writer shared as my recommendation:

> Write down the goals you want to accomplish over the next three months. Maybe you'd like to change jobs or spend more time with family. Now jot down what's stopping you. Is there an activity on your calendar that you agreed to, even though it conflicts with a networking event you wanted to attend? A project you felt obligated to help with although it takes time away from loved ones? The key to an abundant life is saying no to the things that don't drive what you want to say yes to.

Does that sound like you? Do you need to learn to say no to things that don't move you in the direction of your goals? The inability to say no is harder if you don't have a long-sighted view of your life. You feel an internal tug to go in a particular direction, but don't have a reason to act since you haven't captured the vision entirely. For this reason, you take on other people's agendas, and when you see them progressing, you accuse them of monopolizing your time. Here are four reasons why you need a vision statement:

1. It provides focus and motivation.
2. It helps minimize distractions.
3. It guides your daily decisions.
4. It encourages continuous personal and professional growth.

There's no right way to write a personal vision statement. The purpose is to write a brief, compelling statement that speaks to you and calls you to take action. Here are a few sample vision statements:

- Close the assessment achievement gap in science, technology, engineering, and mathematics while increasing college graduation rates and developing leaders in STEM.
- Become an internationally known expert, teacher, consultant and author by helping mid-level, and senior leaders reset mentally through meditation and movement, creating balance and physical abundance.
- Provide inspirational leadership that focuses on employee engagement and extraordinary customer satisfaction that generates a financial gain to stockholders.

MIND
ELEVATION

YOUR VISION STATEMENT

Write a persuasive personal vision statement based on what you want to contribute to the world. Answer the questions below to focus your thoughts. Reference the examples above to help you craft your vision statement.

1. What do I want to happen in the world?
2. Who do I want to become as a result of the impact I want to make?
3. What services do I want to provide?
4. Who needs my services?
5. What happens when I'm a success?

Your Mission Statement

My flight was delayed, my ticket was in my Apple wallet, and I didn't want my battery to die. As I approached the boarding gate, I noticed a casually dressed, middle-aged man sitting alone working on his computer. He appeared friendly, so I made my way over to him. As I moved closer, he looked up and smiled. I smiled back. His non-verbal communication made me feel comfortable so I asked, "Excuse me. Would you mind if I use one of the receptacles behind you to charge my phone?" He happily said, "Yes."

As my battery charged, we struck up a conversation.
I eventually asked, "So what do you do?"
He said, "I'm a dean at a university." Tossing the question back to me he asked, "What do you do?"
I replied, "I help senior leaders increase their income and influence by becoming more likable, marketable, and credible."
He lit up and enthusiastically said, "Oh, wow! I may need your services. I want to become a college president in two years."

What happened in this exchange? What got him excited? He gave me a job title, and I gave him the results I create. It was easy for him to see how I could help him without trying to sell him on what I do. How do you answer the question, "What do you do?" If you answer it the same way he did, your brand probably seems as ambiguous to others as it is to you. Your mission statement communicates to your audience what you help them achieve. It's the ability and promise to solve an issue your audience consistently faces. Delivering on your commitment is what makes you likable (more on this below).

A mission statement is one or two sentences that communicates to the listener what you do, who you serve, and the value people get from your assistance. Crafting a mission statement starts with these simple, yet complex questions: Who am I? Why am I here? What's important to me? What do I want? To accurately respond to these questions, you have to know what they are really asking you.

The Questions

Who am I? I've asked this question to clients and in seminars for years. The response is always the same. People share their titles. I'm a dad, son, brother, and social worker. You've probably been asked this question more times than you can remember, too. Yet, Who am I? still causes you to pause and wonder exactly what it's asking.

I believe the question isn't seeking an answer. The purpose of the question is to excite your curiosity about your significance in the world and to heighten your consciousness that you have a role to play in its evolution. You're dynamic and in continuous motion. While you're pondering the answer to this question and fumbling for the right words to respond, your idea of yourself has evolved.

Why am I here? This question is requesting that you state your purpose: the reason you enter into the presence of your audience. What do you give your audience? What do you help these individuals achieve? Answering those queries puts you on the path to crystalizing your mission.

What's important to me? You have the most prominent role in your transformation. It's contingent on your personal and professional priorities. What you hold close to your heart determines how you make decisions. A list of the matters of the highest importance to you reveals your values and the essentials you need for your well-being.

MIND

ELEVATION

MY ESSENTIALS

Draw a horizontal line in the middle of your page. At the top of the page above the line, write Personal Priorities. At the top just below the line write Professional Priorities. Now, think about what's most important to you. List your personal priorities and professional priorities in their respective locations. Review your lineup. Focus on your top three choices in each category. Respond to the questions, then continue to the next step.

1. Do your personal and professional priorities work together?
2. If not, how are they different?
3. Why are they different?
4. Which priorities are most important to you?

Bring forward your number one ambition from the section Mind Elevation: Identify What You Have, and write it down on a blank sheet of paper. Now compare your priorities to your goal. Are they in sync with one another? If they don't line up, you have to choose another target or reconsider your priorities.

What do I want? Wherever you invest your time and intelligence, you believe, consciously or unconsciously, that there will be a satisfying return on your investment. This question is asking you to define what drives your behavior. What do you want your audience to give you in return for what you give them?

MIND

ELEVATION

WHAT I WANT

Draw a table like the one below. Include the topic headings only. The content in the boxes serves as an example. Fill in your boxes with what you want. Keep the following in mind: Love doesn't have to be romance; recognition could be what you're looking for. Power isn't exclusively influence; it's also a position. Sex isn't necessarily a physical encounter; consider that you need connection. Money isn't only dollars; you may need money to pay for childcare services.

Your answers should consider your priorities.

MONEY	POWER	LOVE	SEX
I want to earn $250,000 a year to give to causes important to me.	I want to influence the direction of employees' careers.	I want the CEO to seek my advice about talent development.	I want to improve the quality of conversations with my spouse.

Your Audience

Your audience is a component of the second step: brand position. However, I'm introducing it now because as you shape your brand package, you need to have an idea of who your audience is. How you present yourself determines the people who are attracted to you. Keep your notes handy from this section; you'll need to review them in the section Position Your Brand.

Your audience is the person, people, or community you want to reach and serve. Before you can help them, you have to understand them. You have to know what they want to accomplish, the barriers to their success, and what they feel as a result of their challenges. Demographics—age, level of education, interests, religious beliefs, and affiliations—also help. This information about your audience helps you to relate, communicate, and connect with them.

DEFINE YOUR AUDIENCE

Identify your audience by completing the blanks:

1. My audiences are_____.
2. My audiences struggle with_____.
3. As a result of not being able to accomplish what's desired, my audiences feel_____.
4. I give my audiences_____.
5. I help my audiences become_____.
6. I help my audiences achieve_____.

My Mission Statement

Now that you've completed the discovery work, you can write your mission statement. Reference your vision statement, priorities, and audience. Here are some sample mission statements:

- To equip businesses and individuals with the tools and techniques needed to interrupt dysfunctional patterns and unwanted and unprofitable behaviors that interfere with decision-making, productivity, creativity, and personal and business success. — Dr. Audrey Sherman, Psychologist, Author, *Dysfunction Interrupted:*

How to Quickly Overcome Depression and Anxiety, Starting Now (dysfunctioninterrupted.com)
- I help students from fourth to eighth grade prepare for academic success by mastering abstract math. — Dr. Kwame Carr, Assistant Superintendent, Author, *Turnaround Principles for Turnaround Principals: Protocols for Creating a Culture of Student Achievement*

WRITE YOUR MISSION STATEMENT

Fill in the blanks below to guide your thinking before writing your mission statement.

I am a _____. As a result of my work, _____. I am known for _____. The world is better because I _____. I'd like to see everyone experience _____.

Your Brand Message

There was a time when family dysfunction, personal weaknesses, and tumultuous life experiences were held close to the chest. Considered private matters, people didn't talk, write, and certainly didn't post such personal messages about themselves on the Internet, since blogging, posting, selfies, and selfie videos didn't exist.

Today, your story, when coupled with invaluable life lessons and inspiration, can become highly sought-after. Music contracts, book deals, and coveted interviews on top television shows are being granted to unknowns, thanks to an intensifying interest in tell-all stories that reveal human vulnerability and strength.

By sharing your story, people feel an instant connection with you. The outcome is you become relatable, and people like that. Your likability factor increases when people think they know you and your story, and feel they can see themselves in it. That's what your brand story is about—connecting you to your audience through relatability. Your brand message has two parts:

1. Your brand story
2. Your brand taglines

Your Brand Story

Most people already have an informal brand story. It's the story you've shared many times around the table at home, at work, or in a restaurant. Your story has at least two characters: a protagonist, which is usually you, and an antagonist (adversary), who is often someone else but can be you.

There's a high point where everything is going as planned and a low point where things go south—and you go with it. Then there's the pivotal moment when things turn, and the pendulum starts to swing the other way. Throughout the story, there are intertwined lessons that explain how you felt, made decisions, and navigated the bumpy terrain. People can see themselves in your story while learning about themselves, life, and others. In the end, you prevail, and although you don't do it alone, you become your own hero.

The brand development process requires you to become conscious of your story and how you tell it. In the past, your purpose for narrating the incident could have been to make people laugh, kill time, or direct people's attention toward you. The principal reason for crafting and sharing a brand story is to reach your audience in a way that evokes a deeper desire to engage with you. It's critical that you get that point. It's imperative because I've had clients who have physically moved beyond the situation, but they tell their story as if they are still in it—and the victim of it. When it's written from that perspective, it's all about you. You'll sound like you need to heal. A well-written brand story pulls your audience in so that they see themselves in you, and you in them.

I've helped clients craft hundreds of captivating brand stories, and the range is as varied as the people on the planet. For example, there's the 40-something lawyer who becomes dependent on his family after a life-threatening stroke. He makes a comeback and uses his story to institute a mental health day for all employees at the company he works. Then there's the 50-something chief of marketing who had a rough ride to the C-suite due to chauvinistic male and envious female co-workers. She commits to mentoring and sponsoring other women—and many are now in senior positions. Conceivably, it could also be the story of a 30-something who was one of the 54 million employees who is bullied on the job. She was fired but vowed to change workplace environments by helping employees see themselves differently. Here's my brand story:

It was a challenging and exciting time in my life. I was in my thirties, and by all accounts, I was successfully leading the public relations team at the university. The only problem: My supervisor had a history of bullying employees, and I wasn't exempt. She'd humiliate me in front of my staff, use unprofessional words to describe me and would tell me how awful a writer I was.

When I followed her instructions to improve my writing, she'd accuse me of submitting someone else's work. Mentally drained and physically exhausted, I sought help from the director of human resources. He wouldn't touch the issue. He asked if I'd be willing to share my experience with the president. I agreed.

During my meeting with the university president, who I thought was an ally, I was reassured that I was doing a great job, and he'd had ongoing complaints about my boss from other employees. He claimed her behavior would not be tolerated. Based on our conversation, I accepted the offer to take two weeks of medical leave, expecting to return to a different work environment.

During my time off, I went to my medical doctor, who diagnosed me as being depressed. He prescribed an antidepressant and suggested I find a job that I'd enjoy. At the time, I didn't think either was necessary since the president made a firm commitment to me that my job was safe. When I returned to work, the president told me they would not be renewing my contract. I couldn't believe what I was hearing. What happened between the time I left and now?

My self-esteem came crashing down. I couldn't figure out how I had gotten to this point. Suddenly I was a student of my own teaching. I was deaf to my own voice. All I could hear were the people in my life whose actions were telling me, "You're not good enough." Every day until my final day at the university, I kept my head up, mouth shut, and at night I cried alone. I didn't know who to trust. Thinking I could have done something differently, I was disappointed in myself and felt embarrassed and betrayed.

Despite what I was thinking, deep inside I knew it was my fight and that only I had the weapons to win. With a flicker of hope, I fought with prayer, affirmations, and the greater vision God had shown me for my life. It was there, in that healing place, that my brand message, "There Is More Inside," was born.

Getting fired led me on a path to seek a higher purpose in my life. It was the right choice because my career skyrocketed to national recognition—including the signing of two book deals and sharing speaking platforms with some of the world's most astute business leaders. Here's where the audience inhales and releases a thunder of applause and victorious cheer:

Eleven years after I was fired, I received a written apology from my former supervisor that praised me for my success and stated,

"No doubt I was dealing with issues that had nothing to do with you."

If I were sharing the story to initiate a conversation about leadership styles or relationship building with employees, I might ask, "What spoke to you in the story?" or "Did you see yourself in the story? If so, where?" If I used it for a keynote presentation, I'd share three things I learned from the experience. The idea is that brand stories teach, engage, and unite audiences.

Now, I want to use this brand story to explain its components and help you craft your own brand story.

1. **Appeal to the masses.** It doesn't matter who you are and whether you've been bullied on your job, you've witnessed a co-worker being mistreated, or know someone who has gone through it. If not, you do now. By mentioning it during the first 15 seconds of the story, it tugs at the heart of the audience evoking compassion and catches their attention. They're drawn in because they know the level of success the speaker has obtained, so they're curious. They want to know what happened and how it was resolved.

   Maybe you don't have a story that nearly everyone can relate to, but in every story, there are certain moments, feelings, and experiences in which most people can connect. Start there. For example, if you're speaking to a younger audience, they may not be able to relate to having a setback due to a health issue, but they can relate to experiencing a loss or trying to make a comeback. The key is to find a point of connection that intrigues your audience while keeping the climax of your story a mystery until the right moment.

2. **Pinpoint the story.** Decide what life or workplace story best connects with your audience. You'll have many different stories from various experiences that will relate to the topic of your

choice and convey the point you want to make. I chose the story above because it's concise, and the audience can see that leadership turned a blind eye to a tyrant. To help you decide, focus on the problem that you assist your audience in solving.

3. **Identify the experience.** Within each story are many experiences and angles of each lesson. For example, the story above could have focused on the turbulent relationship with the supervisor versus the conversation with the president. Another aspect could have looked at the lack of responsiveness from the director of human resources, whose responsibility was to advise the president, oversee the organization's culture, and retain good employees. Remember, the brand message includes who you want to be in the marketplace. To determine the experience you should share, ask yourself, "Who is my audience? What lessons do I want to teach my audience? What action do I want my audience to take as a result of hearing my story?"

4. **Engage, give facts, be vulnerable, and provide a resolution.** Think of your brand story in four sections. You want it to be as crisp as possible. Here are the sections:

Section 1: Engage your audience.

Capture your audience with your opening. In the story above, the first paragraph gives a broad view of what happened and introduces you to the characters. It provokes a desire to know more.

Section 2: Tell the facts of the story.

Notice that paragraphs two and three walk the audience through the core experience of the protagonist and introduce you to a new character: the doctor, a voice of reason; that provides a reasonable option.

Section 3: Be vulnerable.

Invite your audience into your inner thoughts, feelings, or behavior. The purpose is to humanize yourself. Don't cry on their shoulder. Notice the depression diagnosis in paragraph three. This wasn't intended as a sob story; I included it because it communicates to the audience that I am human and transparent about my struggles.

Section 4: Provide a solution.

The final paragraph tells how the main character made it through the personal and professional crisis and, in the end, found success.

5. **Share details that matter.** Don't bore your audience with every detail. Lay out your story so that it moves people through the essence of the experience, not the steps. Notice how I didn't go into detail about why my job was exciting. The reason is this: The story isn't about my success at the university; it's about failed leadership and how the heroine burst forth out of despair.

6. **Close on a high note.** Don't leave your audience caught up in the problem. Bring the story to a resolution with the lessons you've learned. If you're using your story as a discussion tool for employee development, hold the result until your team has had the opportunity to share their perspectives.

CRAFT YOUR BRAND STORY

Use the following outline to develop and craft your brand story:

I. Write the Problem You Help Your Audience Solve
   A. List the different stories relevant to the problem.
   B. Choose the most pertinent story.
   C. Decide on the experience you want to share.

II. Write the Core Message You Want to Convey
   A. Identify the experience that matches the message.
   B. Document the experience.
   C. Pinpoint the areas of the experience that engage the audience, disclose the facts, share your vulnerabilities, and provide a solution.

III. Finalize Your Brand
   A. Organize paragraphs according to sections.
   B. Delete all nonessential text.
   C. Practice and present your brand story.

Your Brand Taglines

Many people who are sitting in front of their family, friends, and co-workers are competing with the sound of beeps from texts, emails, and phone calls, as well as news, social media, and podcast alerts. If they're disregarding the person in front of them, then you can imagine what an enormously difficult task it is to compete for the attention of an overstimulated mind. It's highly probable that if you capture their attention, you've distracted them from something else, and you have only seconds before the next pitch grabs their attention from you.

Your brand story and brand tagline are messages. You use them to direct the attention of individuals in your market toward how you can help them. You increase your chances of maintaining their interest by developing a message from your audience's perspective, and you position it in places where they'll consistently see it. Taglines and quotes are great for this purpose when accompanied by lifestyle video or blogs. I cover how to promote your brand in step three.

Taglines typically complete a thought, answer a question, solve a problem or provide advice. Take Adidas's "Impossible Is Nothing," which offers the idea that "impossible" isn't a concern since it doesn't exist. Chick-fil-A's "Eat Mor Chikin" advises us what to eat, while Burger King's "Be Your Way" (formerly "Have It Your Way") tells you how you can have your meal prepared. SRS Productions, Inc.'s "There Is More Inside" helps you solve the problem of self-defeat by encouraging you to look within for answers.

Brand taglines are optional for employees but must-haves for businesses. However, I read an article about a young advertising executive who developed a slogan that he used on his résumé to showcase his creativity. It worked; he got hired. I've also noticed quotes in employees email signatures. Some departments in large corporations have taglines to augment their presence inside the organization and distinguish themselves while creating a buzz about what they do. A catchy brand phrase is an innovative idea for anyone who dares to step out of the box to get noticed. Plus, it makes for great conversation.

YOUR BRAND TAGLINE

Your tagline should be four words or fewer. Using the questions below, brainstorm possible ideas. You can test them on your friends.

1.   What action do I want my audience to take?
2.   What advice do I want to offer my audience?
3.   What do I want them to know about the quality of my product?
4.   What particular customer service do I provide my audience?
5.   What question is my audience asking that needs an answer?

Your Value

Standing in front of an audience of approximately 500 employees, I asked, "How many people believe they're paid what they're worth?"

No one raised a hand. I then asked, "How many people believe they're worth more than what they're paid?"

Nearly all the people in the room raised their hand. What is the truth? Are they being paid fairly for the value they bring to the organization? How do they know? Like this group of mid-level to senior leaders, I've never spoken to anyone who admitted, "My employer pays me too much money; I'm not worth it." Everyone I know feels slighted when it comes to compensation, yet when I ask them to justify their belief, I get a blank stare.

Your value is as a result of money saved, challenges avoided, or time preserved—in essence, making your customers' lives easier. Who are your customers? Do you know what they need? Can you articulate how you help them achieve their goals? Are you hitting the target according to their expectations? Whether you're an entrepreneur or employee, you have customers, and it's essential that they know what you know that helps obtain success, and what it's going to cost them if you're unavailable.

The Conference Board, a think tank that provides insight into what's ahead in business, polled 800 CEOs about their internal and external concerns. Their number one internal threat: attracting and retaining talent. This fact increases your value if you have the right skills to help solve their problem.

Can you tally how much an organization can profit from your results? Hard to measure, right? Sites like Salary.com, Glassdoor, PayScale, and Vault.com serve as a reference. However, don't let these resources have the final say.

I had a client named Sonia who was an executive assistant and so much more. She sought my help to assist her with communicating her value proposition and negotiating her salary. She aced the interview, and the hiring manager called to make an offer. She wasn't satisfied with the offer, so, as advised, she didn't take it immediately. Instead, Sonia told the hiring manager that she would follow up the next day.

That evening we revisited her value proposition and role-played a likely conversation with the hiring manager. As agreed, Sonia called the manager back. She thanked her for the offer and asked her if she could revisit a few items discussed during the interview. She aligned her skills with high-priority tasks. She also reviewed specific abilities she had that could address some of the concerns expressed about the challenges within the department. The manager was impressed. I received a text from Sonia that read, "They found the money. ☺ Thank you!"

The three biggest mistakes people make during interviews or contract negotiations:

1. Failing to understand and uncover the needs and challenges of the organization

2. Leaving it to the interviewer to align your skills with their tasks
3. Lacking the ability to leverage silence (talking too much)

Your Brand Personality, Persona, and Presence

Have you ever met someone you liked instantly? You didn't know them, but there was something about how they made you feel. You accepted them as genuine and trustworthy. Perhaps you gravitated to them because of their confidence, humor, or intelligence. At the opposite end of this experience, it's possible you've met someone you didn't like. You couldn't put your finger on it, but they seemed peculiar and strange.

According to the American Psychological Association (APA), personality refers to "individual differences in characteristic patterns of thinking, feeling, and behaving." Your personality is your particular way of thinking, being, and behaving that makes you, you! Your personality, your brand identity, is the unique expression of your inner essence, called your persona. Your personality is what people see; your persona is the unseen message that people feel or sense about you.

When your personality and persona are in harmony, you're memorable, and people feel good about you. It becomes how they recognize, connect, and describe you. If they conflict with one another, you leave people perplexed about who you are really. For example, you act confident, but you show signs of insecurity. Or you're smiling, but your body language says you're sad. These conflicting messages are undeniable and impossible to fake even if, at first, others overlook them.

What Makes You Unique

You and another person can draw the same conclusion about a given situation. However, the mental path you took to get there is different. You think, feel, and experience life differently than everyone else on the planet. During the brand development process, a common question is: What makes you unique? The answer: Everything!

The key to differentiating yourself and standing out in a crowd is to carefully examine your experiences, lessons, beliefs, and personal style. You decide how to tell your stories, and market the skills you've mastered. Once you confidently and authentically align your mind, your words and your movement with the truth of who you are, you unapologetically transmit this truth to the world. I'm not advocating you say and do whatever you want whenever you want—that's reckless.

This conversation intends to eliminate the struggle of trying to figure out what makes you unique. Instead, redirect your focus to communicating the unique message that reflects your individuality. People take notice and engage with people who know what advice and qualities make them shine. Having this information is vital to build and sustain confidence, and to become that person your audience is looking for.

MIND

ELEVATION

YOUR PERSONA

Complete the following statements:

1. I am memorable because I_____.
2. The things about my personality that make me engaging are

   _____.
3. People's first impression of me is_____.
4. People's first impression of me is based on

   _____.
5. My personality and persona transmit a similar (or different) message because_____.

Your Presence

According to Jean Baur, career coach and author of *The Essential Job Interview Handbook*, it takes about three seconds for a person who meets you for the first time to determine if they like you and want to do business with you. It's what psychologists classify as "thin slicing."

Accurate or not, it's difficult to grasp that by the time you snap your fingers three times others have evaluated and labeled you. However, it's sobering to recognize the effect your presentation style has on your income and influence. If you pause and think about it, you make quick judgment calls about others, too. What image do you associate with a positive experience? What image causes you to like and trust someone immediately? What image would cause you to shy away from someone?

Your presence is the undeniable message you convey about yourself through your appearance, energy, and composure.

- **Appearance** is your grooming and attire.
- **Energy** is the invisible force that personifies your essence.
- **Composure** is your level of self-assurance. All three work together to guide people's thinking in drawing a positive—or negative—conclusion about you.

HL Larry, a member of the government's Senior Executive Service, says, "If you don't take care of yourself, you won't take care of my business." Isn't it remarkable to know that you own the power to influence people's impression of you and increase your opportunities?

MIND

ELEVATION

YOUR NONVERBAL MESSAGE

Do you want people to take notice that you're in the room? Are you seeking to exude more confidence? Does generating more curiosity about the work you do interest you? You must have a vision of what that looks like before you can get the results you're seeking. Respond to the following questions to help you gain more insight into the image you want to create as well as the changes you need to make to present a more authentic you. Examine the following and document your thoughts about each of them:

1. Describe the perception you want people to have of you.
2. Identify someone you know who best exemplifies the image you want to present.
3. Examine your current outward appearance, energy, and composure. What areas need your attention based on the image you want to project?
4. Write the differences you see in your nonverbal message and that of the person whose style is a prototype.

Your Appearance

In an attempt to meet the demands of the multigenerational workplace, the legal and practical enforcement of workplace attire seems to be changing. Each industry has its policies. I'm not judging what companies permit their employees to wear, but I can remember when you could expect to see bankers in business attire. Men wore a suit and women wore a pant or skirt suit or a dress. Although some bankers still wear suits, I've recently sat across the desk from a male banker dressed in what is now referred to as business casual—khakis and a button-down shirt. For a scheduled meeting, a female small business banker greeted me in tights and a low-cut blouse.

At one time, jeans, tattoos, and piercings were unacceptable. If you had tattoos and piercings, you'd cover them. You understood why this was important to your employer. Today, they're common in some workplace environments. Are the people who want to advance in their careers following this trend?

I was speaking with a 30-something millionaire in the technology industry. We were discussing outward appearance and its impact on one's career. He claimed that conservative companies who don't "get it" and change how they treat Generations Y and Z are going to miss out on recruiting the best talent. For a short time during college, he said, he had a tattoo and plugs, the ear piercing that stretches your earlobes. I didn't see any signs of any of this, so I inquired about them. I'm paraphrasing his response:

Just before graduating college, I started interviewing for jobs. So I took them out and never put them back. My tattoo isn't in a visible place, so that didn't matter.

I didn't seek additional details about the tattoo, but I did ask why he took his plugs out if he firmly believed that companies should allow them. He said, "I outgrew them."

One size doesn't fit all; you have to be clear about your audience. Your audience must accept, or at the very least, not be put off, by your dress style. If your apparel creates unexpressed barriers, it can prolong a buy-in to your message. Worse, your audience may never connect with you. Your attire is your personal preference. After gathering data and weighing your options and risks, decide how you want to dress.

Remember, how you present yourself does determine how others perceive you. Society is becoming more liberal, and some organizations are more lenient, but one thing remains constant: There is a direct correlation between your presentation style and the opportunities you're offered to advance in your career. The point is this: Your attire may look good to you, but it's leadership that has the final say.

I recall being a member of a three-panel television interview. Among us was a psychologist who had a stain on his shirt. That didn't go over well with the producers. They had to find a way to position him and the camera so that viewers couldn't see the spot. After all the work put into concealing it, he was upset when the interviewer only directed one question to him. Do you think that was intentional? Of course, it was.

Regardless of your capability, being less than attentive to every aspect of your presentation signals to management a lack of maturity and the inability to align yourself with the organization's culture. When you fail to do so, it doesn't convey individuality; it communicates resistance.

If you want to know how to dress, look at the person who's in the position you want. I'm not suggesting you copy that person unless you decide it's a look that works for you. I'm encouraging you to look around to read the landscape. A good rule of thumb is to ask yourself, "Is what I'm wearing a distraction?" You can't control anyone's eyes, but you can signal where to look.

MIND

ELEVATION

YOUR BRAND FLAIR

You have a unique personality and style; dress accordingly. However, how do you brand yourself if your audience has many vastly different elements? Let's say you're in human resources during the day and a musician at night. In this case, you have to decide if one career dominates the other. How far do you want to advance in your primary career choice? What are the expectations to consider that will help you get there? Should you have a different style for each career, or is there crossover? Answer these questions to help determine your dress style. Refer to responses of similar questions asked in other Mind Elevation exercises.

1. What is my brand?
2. Who makes up my audience?
3. What is the presentation style of my target market?
4. What role do I want to play in my audiences' life?
5. Will my dress impact opportunities offered to me? If yes, why?
6. Do I need my dress style to add credibility to my message?
7. Do I want to change my dress style?

Your Energy

Being well groomed and wearing the right attire isn't enough. You have to enter the room with an air of confidence and competence. Having the proper posture makes a huge difference in how you're perceived. It's the difference between appearing to be in the game and still trying to become a member of the team.

Your presence is expressed in how you walk and in your body movement. I'm sure you've heard the words vibe, aura, energy, charisma, spirit or finesse. When attempting to read a person, it's likely you've used one of these words to describe the source that's beaming from the person. Energy is your strength and vitality that permeates through your body; it's the thing that communicates liveliness and attitude.

You may be asking: What's the difference between persona and energy? Your persona is what you emanate that others accept as a part of your personality. It can be real or contrived. Your energy is changeable, but not controllable. Let me explain. You can act happy; however, people who read people well can tell you're faking. Dictated by your thoughts, beliefs, and feelings, your energy is the central hub that controls your facial expressions, mannerisms, and behavior. When they aren't in alignment, it signals something's wrong.

Here are five strategies that will boost your energy and communicate a more positive message to others:

1. **Listen to upbeat music.** In 2013, the world was singing, dancing, and clapping to Pharrell William's song "Happy." It lifted us, put smiles on faces, and introduced strangers. In part, the lyrics are:

    > *It might seem crazy what I'm 'bout to say/*
    > *Sunshine she's here, you can take a break/*
    > *I'm a hot air balloon that could go to space/With the air,/*
    > *like, I don't care, baby, by the way/*
    > *Huh, because I'm happy/*
    > *Clap along if you feel like a room without a roof/*
    > *Because I'm happy/*
    > *Clap along if you feel like happiness is the truth/*
    > *Because I'm happy/*
    > *Clap along if you know what happiness is to you/*
    > *Because I'm happy*
    > *Clap along if you feel like that's what you wanna do*

Music makes you move. It will uplift you and put you in tune with your internal rhythm. Use it to calm, energize, or shift you from melancholy to bliss.

2. **Read something good about yourself.** No doubt you've had past successes. Read your bio, a positive performance review, or an encouraging card from a friend. Recalling how much you've accomplished or how much people value what you do will grow your confidence and recharge your memory of how competent and courageous you are.

3. **Draw energy from others.** Have you ever had a problem that you forgot about once you engaged in a conversation with someone? Exchanging ideas with others can give you the surge

of positivity and vitality that swings your attention and energy in the direction of optimism.

4. **Deep breathing.** Genuine gratitude is an excellent way to shift your thinking. Take a deep breath in and hold it for five to 10 seconds. Slowly exhale and mentally repeat the words, Thank You. Feel the negative energy pass through your body, and a new perspective emerge. Repeat these two to three times.

5. **Have fun and play.** I learned this technique in an acting class. The purpose is to get nervous energy to pass through you. Stretch your fingers apart. Lift and hold them in front of your face with your palms facing toward you. Take in a deep breath and begin to move your fingers until they're moving like a dance before your eyes while simultaneously saying Ah! until you've released the breath you took. Repeat.

Your Walking Style

I was a model for ten years. During that time, I strutted down runways at high-end department stores and pivoted on the set of the QVC Network, the home shopping channel. I've worked with hundreds of beautiful women and handsome men. Each had their unique style of walking. So what were designers looking for? Looks? Height? Weight? These were factors they took into consideration, but most often the models who worked full time in the business walked with confidence and exuded a positive attitude.

You don't have to be a model to transmit confidence and competence. I've defined four walking types, which one closely resembles your style? Which one would you most like to project?

The Politician. When you walk into a room, people know it. Your strides are wide, and your pace fast. Your head is up and shoulders back, you appear confident. You make eye contact with as many people as possible. You never meet a stranger. Regardless of who passes you, you greet them. Your personality and presence are magnetic and attract attention.

The Executive. Your presence communicates power. Appearing poised, you walk smoothly and deliberately. Your head is up, and your posture straight as your eyes scan the room. You're an observer who is friendly but not familiar. Eye contact yields a nod and a warm but partial smile. Conversations with you are short but purposeful. Your personality and presence are calming, and they generate respect.

The Celebrity. You walk in a room, and all eyes are on you. Elegant, you glide with flair and grace. Well-groomed, your perfect posture and controlled pace create a buzz. People are wondering, "Who is that?" Your personality and presence are inspiring, which sparks interest. However, your charisma doesn't always translate into business or job opportunities.

The Observer. You quietly enter the room and stroll cautiously around with your head slightly tilted down. Your shoulders are rounded, and your eyes drift between the floor and random room scans. You appear timid, and your arms are firmly at your side or folded across your body. Your shy demeanor is interpreted as withdrawn, causing you to be overlooked. Your personality and presence are standoffish, which causes low engagement.

MIND

ELEVATION

IDENTIFY YOUR WALKING STYLE

What message do you transmit when you walk into a room? Do people smile naturally and make their way to you? Do people avoid you? How you walk is a factor in determining whether people think you are someone they should know. Identify your walking style:

- I'm like the politician; I'm popular. I engage with everyone, even when I'm on the run. I sometimes miss opportunities because people view me as a happy person.
- I'm like the executive; I don't miss much. I'm clear on why I'm there, and I get what I want. People are sometimes afraid to approach me.
- I'm like the celebrity; people notice me and engage with me. I don't always make the impact I prefer because people don't see my real value.
- I'm like the observer; I'm shy and not a fan of intimate social situations. I'm friendly and polite. People would see how intelligent I am if they'd stop and have a conversation with me.

Do you need to shift your presence to communicate a more positive attitude through your posture and walking style? Here's my three-step strategy. Transform your presence using these tips:

Step 1: Pay attention to your facial expression. Share a warm, inviting facial expression. Don't try to control your facial expression; instead, control how you feel about yourself, others, and the current experience. By managing your thoughts and maintaining a positive attitude, your eyes and facial expression will work collaboratively to light up a room.

Step 2: Look people in the eyes and greet them. Nothing will skyrocket your personal and professional success more than being present and aware of what's going on around you. Make eye contact with people and greet them with the warmth that comes from giving people what they deeply yearn for—acknowledgment! When appropriate, while making eye contact and flashing a welcoming smile, shake their hand firmly. Don't make awkward moments more awkward. If they have something in their hands, maintain eye contact and say, "I see your hands are full. It's a pleasure to meet you." Or, if you have a cold, don't transfer it to others. Just say, "I'm sorry; I shouldn't shake your hand because I have a cold." They'll thank you.

Step 3: Improve your posture. You may unconsciously slouch while sitting at a desk typing on a computer for hours or looking down as you text. Consider the following to improve your posture:

- Hold your mobile device at eye level when you check your email or text messages. This will automatically force your head and neck into an upright position, versus stretching those muscles downward as you hold it closer to your lap.
- Strengthen your internal core by working out regularly. A strong core supports your upper body and keeps you from slouching.
- Commit to deep-breathing exercises. As you take a breath, you'll naturally pull your belly button toward your spine. This strengthens your core, elongates your neck, and automatically pushes your shoulders into the correct position.

IMPROVE YOUR POSTURE

Years ago, I was a certified instructor for Barbizon International. At a local modeling school, I taught students how to stand to achieve perfect posture. To start, practice the following steps in front of a mirror. Then repeat this exercise wherever you are; it will immediately boost your confidence and appearance of competence.

Practice the following steps to improve your posture:

Step 1: Plant your feet shoulder-width apart on the floor.

Step 2: Distribute your weight evenly between your legs.

Step 3: Keep your knees slightly bent.

Step 4: Gently pull your belly button toward your spine; you'll feel your spine lengthen and straighten as you do this.

Step 5: Keep your head and neck in line with your shoulders and your chin parallel to the floor.

Another quick tip (I did this when I was in the entertainment industry): Balance a book on your head and walk around at home for 10 minutes a day. It works!

Composure Reveals Your Character

Competitors are on your heels, good employees are exiting, and you're running out of innovative ideas to navigate a difficult time in the company's history. As a member of the leadership team, you're expected to have answers to complex questions that will stop the bleeding and grow the organization.

In the face of adversity and overwhelming odds, it's easy to be swept away by the mental, emotional, and physical drain of your leadership role, and the expectations placed on you. I bet you've witnessed leaders who aren't skilled at putting challenges in perspective, rallying their team, or creating collaborative partnerships. They yell, throw things, and lash out at their team members. You'd prefer to avoid them because you never know what to expect from them.

Composure is the ability to maintain internal and external calm during chaos. It's during these times that effective, levelheaded leaders exhibit poise and discipline over themselves and their emotions. It takes maturity, experience, and wisdom to be directed by sound judgment and discretion.

Linda was president of a U.S. sales division and a tremendous asset to the billion-dollar company. Management much appreciated her work ethic, drive, and ability to supersede sales goals. However, she became the topic of discussion in the boardroom when complaints of her bullying behavior and intimidation tactics reached the CEO. Her competence and executive presence were now in question.

When called into the boardroom and asked about her behavior, she blamed others and gave excuses to justify her actions. Her reasoning was not accepted. The executive team told her she needed to control her temper and become the leader the position demanded, or her services would no longer be needed. They allowed her to build her skills by working with an executive coach. Through coaching, she learned how to manage herself and her emotions. Growing her composure and executive presence, she later became a CEO. Here's how she did it:

Develop composure. You don't wake up one day and feel serenity. Developing an even-tempered demeanor is the result of years of training yourself to take hold of yourself and your emotions when you feel your heart pounding, blood pressure rising, and stomach churning. Gaining composure over yourself is a self-study of what triggers you and what causes you to misfire.

Patiently listen. In my book, *5 Steps to Assertiveness: How to Communicate With Confidence and Get What You Want,* Step Two recommends that you "listen assertively." Listening is a skill few people learn, and even fewer people master. Listening isn't a skill that is taught, yet people are disciplined when they fail to hear and understand what's being communicated.

When you were growing up, how many times did an adult give you instructions, and try to verify that you understood what was being asked of you? Once? Twice? Never? Did your parents accuse you of not listening, but never confirmed with you that you understood what was being asked? They assumed you understood the command and you made a choice not to follow it.

When you communicate, how many times do you confirm with your listeners that they understand what you're saying? How many times do you confirm with the speaker you know what they're saying?

There are a lot of assumptions in the communication experience, and most of them are incorrect. When you communicate, you speak according to your educational background, life experiences, and perspectives—often not recognizing that the other person has his own unique experiences, too. The result is facts are left out, and too many put in—causing tension and confusion in the communication experience.

Rushing a conversation by interrupting the speaker or making assumptions about what the person is going to say triggers misunderstandings and conflicts. Stay present in the discussion, slow down, and listen so that you understand and speak to be understood. Ask and receive clarifying questions. You can confirm that you understand the speaker's message by repeating what you hear. Consider "Are you saying…" or "This is what I'm hearing…" Assess you and your team's communication connection with the following mindset elevation.

MIND
ELEVATION

YOUR COMMUNICATION CONNECTION

During your next staff meeting or gathering of family and friends (five is a good number), share a specific task you want to be completed and how. Tell them to write down your request as they understand it. Now ask each employee to tell you what you're asking them to do. Only one person speaks at a time, and that person must share what they've written on their paper. If you discover that everyone doesn't have the same response, follow up with this exercise.

Use the same people. This is important because often we label people as being poor listeners, slow learners, or insubordinate. Allow each person an opportunity to share what they understand is expected of them. Let them ask questions. Time the process. Ask the group if they think it saved time, eliminated mistakes, and increased their confidence in completing the project.

In rushed environments, taking time to communicate effectively can seem too time-consuming. But remember that old adage, "Haste makes waste." Here's some tip on how to communicate like an executive:

Differentiate between what's yours and theirs. Many people don't know how to organize their thoughts and succinctly communicate them. They go off on tangents, take the conversation off course, and consume time. Life would be easier if you could avoid them, but you can't. Learning to keep the conversation on task and moving it forward respectfully maintains focus and increases productivity. Help the speaker by acknowledging what you hear, and separating your responsibilities, the speaker's obligations and what has to be worked on together to reach the goal. This approach retains your power and poise while positioning you as the leader.

Decipher the facts. Exceptional leadership is being able to make critical and timely decisions that have a positive impact on people and profits. Detach yourself from your preconceived notions regarding where you want to go and how you want to get there. Listen to the facts, weigh the risks, and decide the direction.

Engage people, not personalities. Every person has their reason for working the way they do. It becomes apparent in their behavior and choices that they have a hidden agenda. They look for people who agree with them, and together they work in silos. Don't get dragged into private agendas, emotions, and dysfunctional personality patterns. Look to the strategic plan to guide your choices and the direction of the organization.

YOUR CRITICAL DECISION-MAKING SKILLS

Respond true or false to the following statements:

1. My opinions of others don't cloud my judgment.
2. I don't let my emotions get in the way of my decision.

3. I consider other people when deciding; however, I focus on long-term results.
4. I'm not an impulsive decision maker, yet it doesn't take me long to decide.
5. I seek the opinion of others, yet accept the responsibility for my decision.
6. I quickly weigh the facts, trust my gut, and decide.
7. I'm okay if everyone doesn't agree with my decision.
8. I don't keep questioning myself after I decide.
9. If I don't get the results I expect from my choice, I learn the lesson and move on.
10. I often hear other people say, "You make good decisions."

If you answered true to all 10 statements, you're an excellent decision-maker. If you answered true to eight or nine comments, you're good at making decisions. If seven and below were true for you, observe yourself more often. Examine how and why you make your choices and adjust as necessary.

Your Likability Factor

I was failing miserably, and I felt the impact in my fading confidence. In 2010, I learned the most important lesson about branding—it's more than a great product with a well-crafted, captivating message.

I had 90 days to engage a community around a new brand. I chaired the board of a new scholarship fund, and we raised $16,000 in six weeks from a grassroots effort of community contributions. We received an additional $2,000 over the next six months. According to experts in the field, the numbers were extremely encouraging. So I decided we'd host our first major fundraiser.

I crafted the vision and mission statements that would unite people and champion a worthy cause. I wrote an inspirational brand story and a concise message to inspire engagement. Plus, I established a value proposition to promote the emotional satisfaction gained from helping others.

After building the brand, I reached out to Emmy Award–winning journalist Byron Pitts, who was a *60 Minutes* correspondent at the time. The message in his book, *Step Out on Nothing*, would form the perfect partnership. My pitch worked, and he agreed immediately to headline the event. I was personal friends with award-winning journalist and Comcast Network television host, Arthur Fennell. I recruited him to serve as master of ceremonies. Two recognizable names and faces would provide unique marketing value and instant credibility.

A newcomer to fundraising, I reached out to seasoned veterans for help. Impressed with my brand strategy, they gave me advice, guidance, support, and referrals. They suggested I use their name to secure appointments with key corporate decision makers. Enthusiastic about the potential, I started booking appointments.

During every meeting with corporate decision-makers, I heard the same thing, "You have an impressive brand strategy." As one vice president of marketing at a bank put it, "It's one of the best combinations of branding and marketing I've seen in my 30-plus years in the business." Potential corporate funders loved the story, were impressed with our short-term success, and couldn't believe Byron Pitts had agreed to participate in our unproven but praiseworthy event. Ultimately, they were not comfortable donating to an event with no history.

Have you ever been in similar shoes? You're prepared for the meeting, have a knock-it-out-of-the-park presentation, and an initial positive response that ends with, "Good job, but sorry I can't help you." It was disheartening, but I was in too deep to stop.

With little time left to secure corporate sponsors, I had to rethink the direction of our brand strategy. How could the scholarship become more credible without a track record? I realized the brand wasn't enough. I needed inside influencers who personally knew, liked, and trusted me. I tapped into my professional network. That decision was pivotal. They introduced me to their friends, and the brand started to breathe.

Our first corporate sponsor signed 30 days before the event. By the date of the event, M&T Bank, Walmart, Delmarva Power, and Computer Aid, Inc. (CAI) were on board. WBOC-TV of Maryland, our media sponsor, and Smith Masonry, Inc., were the first responders. In addition, nine reception hosts made a 500-dollar minimum contribution, and 300 tickets and over 200 copies of Byron's books were sold. It was a raving success! This accomplishment was a direct result of two things that support the importance of the likability factor:

1. My brand, which offered credibility to the new brand
2. Existing relationships with power players who used their political capital to influence decision-makers who manage and contribute money

The results tell us that decision-makers do hesitate to fund new events, but it doesn't stop them from contributing to an event. What exactly were the decision-makers saying to me? You have a great message, but I don't know you and, therefore, I don't like or trust you. Don't get me wrong; they didn't dislike me either. They didn't know me, so they were neutral.

It's likely you've also benefited from someone who recommends you by creating an opening for you to advance. Without endorsements, the door remains closed—and you're standing on the other side of it. That's what a job reference is, a stamp of approval that you're okay to let in the door. People endorse people they know, like, and trust.

MIND

ELEVATION

ARE YOU LIKABLE?

In every relationship, you're liked for one reason: your ability to successfully satisfy a need in the person's life. When your value dwindles, so does the interest of the person with whom you have a relationship. You can increase your likability factor when you know why people like you. Discover what makes you likable by completing the following statements.

I am likable because I am_____.

These qualities help people to_____.

Most often I hear people say I am_____.

My desired likability factor is_____.

I need to change the following to increase my likability factor

_____.

Communication Style

There's a quote that many people repeat, "People will forget what you said, people will forget what you did, but people will never forget how you made them feel." My experience is this: What you say, how you say it, and what you do determines how people feel. Here, I provide information to awaken you to the branding essentials needed for a positive communication experience. Your brand speaking style is what influences who engages with you and why. Before I go into detail, I want to discuss some communication styles so you can identify where you fit.

There are four general styles of communication: passive, passive-aggressive, aggressive, and assertive. You may be a passive communicator who lets things go unchallenged, a passive-aggressive who lets things go while you lay low and wait to attack the unsuspecting, an aggressive communicator who forcefully challenges others, or an assertive communicator who consciously enters into the unspoken communication agreement. Regardless of where you are on the continuum, you can move closer to the center and become the ideal assertive communicator.

Here are brief descriptions of the different types of communication styles to help you to determine better where you fit.

Passive. Do you have a pattern of deliberately avoiding conflict by withholding your opinions, feelings, and ideas from others? Are you left feeling invisible because you ignore your needs? Passive communicators are fearful of setting well-defined boundaries, and as a result, have their rights and personal space violated.

Passive-Aggressive. Do you refuse to address problems when they occur? Do you lash out without warning? Passive-aggressive communicators appear to be cooperative, but snide remarks and unexpected malicious attacks expose what they're thinking. Undealt with feelings of disregard causes them to sabotage their career opportunities and relationships.

Aggressive. Do you attack or blame others for what happens? Have you been criticized for not taking responsibility for your actions? Aggressive communicators tend to have a low threshold for listening, triggering repeated interruptions while others are talking. Among other types of behavior, they use the volume of their voice to incite fear or specific words to control the behavior of others.

Assertive. You enter into conversations consciously aware that it's a privilege to communicate with another human being. You understand that they have rights and responsibilities during the communication experience, and so do you. You respect and honor the thoughts, feelings, and opinions of others and your own.

Here's a partial list of rights and responsibilities taken from the comprehensive list in my book, *5 Steps to Assertiveness: How to Communicate with Confidence and Get What You Want*:

You and those you interact with have the right to:

- Have your own opinion
- Excuse yourself from an unpleasant, contentious exchange
- Be listened to without interruption
- Express your needs

- Draw your conclusion

With rights come responsibilities. Individuals who engage in a conversation have the responsibility to:

- Be honest
- Make a genuine effort to understand the speaker's needs
- Accept the person as they are
- Listen without judgment
- Seek agreement whenever possible

YOUR COMMUNICATION STYLE

Identify which statement you most identify with, and match it to the communication style below.

1. My thought is this: Why say anything? People aren't going to listen anyway.
2. I like to tell it like it is; if people can't accept the truth then shame on them.
3. I'd prefer to show people what I mean instead of telling them since that's the only time they'll listen to me.
4. I believe communication is a privilege; it's an opportunity to express my opinion, and I appreciate hearing another person's perspective.

1 = a passive communicator
2 = aggressive speaker

3 = passive-aggressive

4 = assertive

The Speaking Branding Assessment

Dynamic communicators are more than assertive speakers, compassionate listeners, and effective negotiators. They know how to use the combination of language, tone, and words to elicit specific responses. When you use the brand model components mission, message, and value, you'll operate from a framework that leverages the branding process. This approach delivers an intentional message that has intellectual and emotional appeal—stirring a reaction in your audience.

I've developed a brand communication model with five key components that give you an edge in the communication exchange. I'm not referring to a competitive edge. I'm talking about an advantage over your past behavior that can no longer help you move forward.

Keep the following in mind: The communication experience is a process of continuously listening to others and sharing ideas while negotiating to have your needs met. It is likely you don't communicate the same way all the time. With whom you're speaking and when, along with your temperament and that of the other person, affect what you say and how you say it. Revisiting the idea of composure is a good reminder to slow down and pay attention to yourself, and to what you're creating in the moment.

The Mission. Whether you're communicating to persuade a team to follow your lead or telling a joke to lift the heaviness in a room, every word you speak plays a role in linking you and your audience. Your reason for sharing thoughts determines the words you choose and where you place them. The meaningful way in which you share your thoughts determines whether people will listen to you and drives why they listen. Think of your word choices as stimuli for your audience.

YOUR COMMUNICATION MISSION

To determine your mission in the communication experience, ask your-self these questions:

1. Who am I having a conversation with?
2. What is the purpose of this conversation?
3. Why am I entering into this conversation?
4. What do I want my audience to think, feel, and do?

The Message. The message is the tone you use to awaken emotion in your audience. It tells people what you want them to know and how you want them to feel in the moment. The strength with which you present your words expresses your core opinion of the person to whom you're speaking and your mood at the time of delivery—signaling to listeners whether it's safe to be with you.

YOUR COMMUNICATION MESSAGE

Use the message to define what emotion you want to stir within your audience. Your response to the next three questions will help you decide:

1. What impression do I want my audience to have of me?
2. How can I leave my desired impression?
3. How will I use my tone to manage my message?

The Value. You speak to be heard, and hope you're understood. You share information with hopes that it's useful to the listener. But what you think a person needs to hear may be far from what they want to hear. As a result, people check in and out of conversations based on their interest in the speaker and how relevant the information is to them. Is there a way to grab someone's attention and maintain it regardless of whether the subject interests them? Of course there is.

I'm sure you can recall a time when someone was talking about a subject that wasn't intriguing, but how the person presented the information was. You locked onto every word, believing he would eventually say something you could use. How you articulate your ideas and enunciate your words stimulate interest. The fluidity and the rhythm with which you speak keep your audience listening and wanting to stay mentally engaged with you.

FINDING YOUR RHYTHM

Here's a tactic that I was taught early in my acting career: Practice reading nursery rhymes to find your rhythm. It sounds elementary, but it's a secret weapon that many actors and speakers use to find and develop their rhythm. Now, respond to the next three questions:

1. What am I going to say that adds value to my audience?

2. How will I leverage my internal rhythm and presence to maintain the attention of my audience?

3. How can I use words to keep listeners interested in what I have to say?

The Reaction. Every time you communicate, you're seeking a response. Responses don't have to be verbal; they can be an action that you want the other person to take. Your volume is how loud you choose to state your point.

While facilitating a full-day workshop for female mid-level to senior leaders, an attendee proudly stated, "I deliberately speak softly during meetings to force people to lean in and listen to me." My first thought was, "Why would she diminish her confidence and authority to present herself as soft-spoken and cautious." So I asked, "How does your team perceive you when you do that?" She was stunned by the question. After a long pause, a colleague chimed in, "I would perceive that person as nervous and uncertain. And I know she's neither."

On the other end of the spectrum, when you combine high volume, firm tone, and rapid rhythm, people can perceive you as being angry and inflexible. This could cause them to shut down and draw a false conclusion about you and how it would be to work with you.

It's best to be somewhere in the middle. When you need to make a vital point that requires people to be alert, you can call for the audience's attention by telling them you're about to say something of great significance and meaning to you. By being vulnerable and by concisely revealing your emotional state, the listener moves out of judgment and opens themselves up to connecting with you while trying to understand what you're saying on all levels—mentally, emotionally, and intellectually. You can also use this technique when people's eyes begin to look shiny and glazed over.

YOUR COMMUNICATION REACTION

Do you know the reaction you're seeking from your audience? Now is the time to uncover it. Reflect and respond to the next two questions:

1. What is the ideal response I'd like to get from my audience?
2. What can I do to provoke that response?

The Platform. We've already covered how your nonverbal communication sets the stage for your brand's success. Your dress, presence, posture, facial expressions, hand movements, and other gestures are all forms of nonverbal communication. In the communication experience, what you say before you speak creates an opening to enter into the hearts of your audience. Your presentation and presence extend an invitation to enter your world and establishes whether your audience feels, sees, and hears: Welcome!

YOUR BRAND'S PLATFORM

Think about the conversation we've had up to this point, and answer the following questions.

1. What adjustments do you need to make in your communication style?
2. How will the changes improve your audience's perception of you?
3. What will you get for the changes you make?

Study this table to understand how the process works.

The Mission	My reason for talking is to	inspire people to see what's inside them.
The Message	The emotions I want to provoke are	excitement, urgency, and confidence.
The Value	The relevance of my message is	people want to understand themselves and their capacity for success.
The Reaction	The reaction I desire is	gratitude.
The Platform	I will be perceived as	a role model.

Fill your responses in the empty column of the table below.

The Mission	My reason for talking is to	
The Message	The emotions I want to provoke are	
The Value	The relevance of my message is	
The Reaction	The reaction I desire is	
The Platform	I will be perceived as	

Executive Presence

He replaced his brand attire—a T-shirt and jeans—with a suit and tie when called by Congress to review Facebook's mishandling of user data. No matter your perspective on the issue, for billionaire Mark Zuckerberg it was time to present himself to the world as an executive. But did he exhibit executive presence? Before we delve into executive presence, I want to shatter misconstrued notions about what it is.

Misconceptions of Executive Presence

Even without executive presence, you can still earn certain perks that can make it look like you have it. But isn't it holistic success that you want? Executive presence is not:

- **An image**. True or false, the purpose of an image is to control what others believe and accept about you. An image that's created to impress people and control their opinion of you rather than communicate an accurate picture of who you are does not signal executive presence.

- **Position, power, and popularity.** Most people are drawn to power. We're intoxicated with the perks of a high-ranking job and the fame that comes with it. We've also witnessed far too many times that people who possess position, power, and popularity can have their lives ruined. For this reason, you aren't automatically endowed with executive presence as a result of extraordinary success.

- **Inflated confidence.** Having an air of confidence is different from having actual confidence. You should have faith in yourself, in others, and in what you believe can happen. However, when your confidence is overblown, and you fail to see the full picture and the impact of your decisions on all people, you've missed achieving executive presence.

- **Money.** Money can come into your life in various ways: hard work, inheritance, marriage, an accident, or luck. Acquiring wealth creates an opportunity to do things you haven't done before, but it doesn't give you executive presence.

What is Executive Presence?

There was a buzz in the air. We had prepared with great anticipation for the arrival of Iman, the beautiful supermodel, actress, and entrepreneur. After viewing photos of models, she handpicked five of us to launch her makeup line on QVC. I felt honored, surprised to have been chosen, and anxious to meet her.

As she walked into the room, we gravitated toward her radiance, confidence, and poise—her executive presence. She was friendly, but not familiar. Her persona was gracious, yet very commanding. I literally said to myself, "There are models, and then there are models. She's a model."

Several years later, I was on the set of the movie, *Beloved*. Oprah and her assistants were walking back up the hill to her trailer. I impulsively yelled, "Oprah!" She stopped, turned around, and looked down the hill. I ran toward her. Composed, she waited for my arrival. As I approached her, I could feel the strength and power of her presence. She was balanced, welcoming, and authentic. As I nervously spoke, she looked me in the eyes, affectionately invited me into her personal space and wrapped her arms around me. She whispered, "You're going to be okay. You're going to do well." After we parted company, her energy and words of encouragement lingered with me, perhaps influencing my business development decisions.

One such decision was to become an ambassador for the U.S. Air Force as an honorary commander. In this role, I advocated for and supported the only port mortuary for dignified transfers of U.S. fallen military members on foreign soil. I enjoyed opportunities to speak to our military and found it fascinating to learn how they develop leaders.

Here's an example: In 30 minutes, his motivational speech was over. He stepped off the stage, and the crowd swarmed around him. I stepped back and observed how he interacted with each person. Once the line dispersed, I made my way over to introduce myself. I must have been at least the 200th person he had spoken with that day, but the 20th Chief of Staff for the U.S. Air Force General Mark Anthony Welsh, III, was gracious, present, and attentive. With a firm handshake and penetrating eye contact, he was alert, knowledgeable, and an exceptional listener. His attire, demeanor, and communication skills were all credible signs of executive presence.

All of the individuals I've just mentioned are leaders in their fields and the embodiment of executive presence. Notice they don't express it the same way; nevertheless, they share some commonalities such as an elevated persona that radiates self-awareness and mental agility. Iman, Oprah, and General Welsh are poised and proven leaders who blend and balance astute business acumen and immense emotional intelligence while being able to exhibit calm confidence, authentic connection, and trustworthy competence.

That's executive presence: the measure of who you are that sets unspoken boundaries and expectations of how to interact with you while welcoming people into your space. Who do you know that exhibits executive presence? What do you see in them that assures you they personify executive presence?

Although difficult to put into words, and even more challenging to develop, executive presence isn't exclusive to any one person. Anyone open and willing to do the work can learn how to harness their energy, regulate their emotions, and control their behavior. It starts by understanding you're head honcho, the commander and chief of *you*!

When you're looking at executive presence in someone else, it starts with their outward appearance. Sylvia Ann Hewlett, author of *Executive Presence: The Missing Link Between Merit and Success*, says that "appearance is our filter." This is true when we are looking at others. However, when you're building executive presence, it begins with understanding your internal dynamics and remodeling yourself from the inside out. See the illustration (next page).

Since you're reading this book, it's likely you've been on a journey of self-improvement for a while. We've been doing the foundational

EXECUTIVE PRESENCE

CONFIDENCE COMPETENCE
ELEVATED
PERSONA
COURAGE

SELF-ACTUALIZATION

PERSONA • APPEARANCE •
MINDSET • ATTITUDE
PRESENCE
BELIEFS
PERSONALITY • SELF-ESTEEM •
VALUES

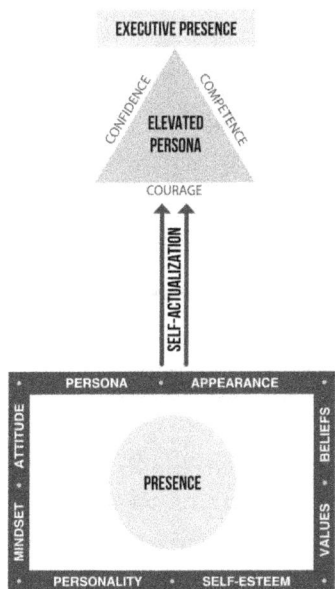

work together since you opened this development tool. You'll advance to self-actualization when you become more aware of your internal dynamics, behavior, and pain points. Pain points are memories of past experiences or events that, when seen again or pushed, resurface and cause you to react unexpectedly. Being accountable for and managing your life, even if everything that has happened to you isn't your fault, is the only way to walk through the demands of self-actualizing.

Self-actualization is being an expert in knowing, understanding, managing, and loving yourself, not in a narcissistic way, but in a manner that recognizes you attract what's in you, and you give others what you give to yourself. Reaching that level of courage to be yourself, the confidence to respect and accept others, and the competence to deliver on your performance promises, elevate your internal persona and transmit executive presence!

Without words, executive presence communicates you're an invaluable resource, and it's worthwhile to have a conversation with you. Exclusive of having to sell yourself, or demand respect, your persona emanates admiration. Proficiency is the space that people sense between executive presence and them. Executive presence is infused with intelligence, temperament, inspiration, and influence to advance a strategic vision like this—I'm a courageous, confident, and competent leader.

Elevate Your Executive Presence

After spending a decade in the image-driven entertainment industry, I decided to accept an invitation to interview for a recruiter position at a university. Although I was thankful for the opportunity, within weeks it was evident that I had grossly underestimated my skills, knowledge, abilities, and the value they brought to the position.

Not only did I know I could be a more significant contributor to the institution, but my track record was evidence of the same. Instead of gossiping about students, staff, faculty, and administration, I listened to the problems they complained about, and why the challenges concerned them.

During the observation period, I did my job. I implemented new recruitment tools and strategies that led to history-making success. I created alliances with senior leaders, accepted projects outside my job description, and made myself visible at on-campus and other networking events.

After assessing my skills and experiences and examining problems, I identified several I could fix. Within six months of working on campus, I pitched an idea to the assistant to the president that would boost morale and employees' skills—an on-campus training center for employees. The assistant appreciated my suggestion and requested a proposal.

Before I could fulfill the request, the director of public relations resigned and I received a call to consider the position. After going through the interviewing process, I accepted the offer. Within a year of taking the recruiter position, I moved into my new role.

As director of public relations, I had a seat at the table in the president's cabinet and attended administrative council meetings every Monday morning. I provided updates and advised the president and senior leaders on all the internal and external issues that would impact the image and brand of the institution. When I saw the president at events, he'd pull me aside to solicit additional insights regarding the university.

Not only did this role give me a seat in the C-suite, but it also allowed me to lead a dynamic public relations team that made history and was recognized by the board of trustees. Your brand builds trust; your executive presence confirms it.

I didn't share that story to impress you, but to impress upon you that if I could get to the C-suite, you're fully capable of getting leadership to notice you, too.

Your Brand and Executive Presence

You've done a lot of work assessing and developing your brand so far. Here's a quick recap of the fundamentals covered earlier and how they translate into the foundation you need to build your executive presence:

1. **Manage your mind.** Chapter One provided you with content and mind-elevation exercises to help you shift your mindset. Everything begins in your mind. How you perceive and interpret information about yourself and others are at the core of how you present yourself. Being aware of your thoughts, your behavior, and the impact of both will help shape your presence. When you display executive presence, people will leave your company feeling good about who they are.

2. **Develop the right attitude.** Evidence of your views show up in everything you do. There's an appeal to showing a positive, enthusiastic, bubbly, and attentive demeanor. But I want to caution you: The stance when operating with executive presence is pleasant and supportive at polite distances. As a leader, this formula keeps your judgment objective and your decisions impartial.

3. **Match your personality and persona.** Your persona is the invisible, yet unmistakable energy you transmit, while your character is how you express that energy. Inconsistencies don't go unnoticed, so how you dress and act during brief encounters will not fool people if you can't maintain your behavior during long-term exchanges. Executive presence signals a calm, confident temperament that's developed over time.

4. **Be attentive to your outward appearance.** How you dress and wear your hair is your choice. If you want to set the stage for your success and communicate you are a leader, you need

to present yourself as polished and poised. Mark Zuckerberg made a good move by wearing a suit when he spoke to Congress. When appropriate, a well-designed, well-made suit or dress says, "I'm credible. Take me seriously. I'm here to conduct business."

5. **Purposeful carriage and communication.** The way you walk and move about in a room tells people that you're someone they should know. Your self-assurance is revealed in your pace, strides, and posture. Executive presence is when you don't linger too long in any one place, and your steps are intentional. No meaningless small talk, you're on a mission to observe, learn, and decide where people fit, and how to advance the organization.

6. **Communication.** How you engage in the communication experience is critical to how people perceive you and your abilities. Executive presence is the next level of understanding that your language is crisp and your empathy apparent. How you frame what you say is done with the courage to say it, the confidence to know how to say it, and the competence to know when to say it.

7. **Clarity of role and purpose.** Having a brand gets you seen and heard, while executive presence is the added asset—your secret weapon—needed to leverage your brand. Executive presence doesn't say you won't have moments that scare you. It does mean you've mastered looking at the target and can stay grounded in chaotic environments while conceiving and implementing a plan to lean in and excel.

Developing Executive Presence

The purpose of developing executive presence isn't to force you to conform to any standard. Remember the earlier examples of Iman, Oprah, and General Welsh? Each has a unique personality, persona, and style of displaying executive presence. You, too, can authentically personify executive presence based on your personality and style—and purpose. That's why I've combined personal brand development with executive presence. Once you build the structure of your brand and executive presence, you'll have the tools to grow and can adjust later as needed. Keep in mind how you process information, prepare for meetings, interact with people, communicate, and present yourself determines whether you have executive presence.

Develop yourself in the following areas:

Level up your mind. There's a difference between being a positive thinker and having a solid grip on yourself, life, and people. Mindset growth begins with perfecting your attitude. To develop a mindset in alignment with executive presence, you have to tackle and overcome adverse situations that disrupt your thought patterns and interfere with your emotional well-being.

Your subjective interpretation of the event causes external events to disturb your peace. You can only stabilize yourself by knowing your triggers and how to manage them. You can achieve this by recognizing what's happening when it's happening. Instead of resisting and trying to overcome them, develop a management strategy by changing how you see the world, which will change how the world sees you.

TRACK YOUR TRIGGERS

Become aware of what's going on inside you to identify your internal barriers and what triggers them. I'm referring to the pain points I spoke of earlier. Learning what they are and why you have an unpleasant reaction to them will help you manage and possibly outgrow them. Use this mindset elevation as a game. Talk to and laugh at yourself. We all have pet peeves that get to the best of us but are not as serious as we think. Here are the steps to embrace your triggers and make improvement. Have fun with this.

Step 1: Pick an issue. Choose one situation you want to work on that needs your immediate attention. Don't fall into the trap of over-committing yourself to two or three simultaneously. You want to see improvements in your behavior through small, consistent changes.

Step 2: Take note of yourself, the people, and the situation. Pay attention when your blood pressure starts rising and irritation is getting the best of you. Identify what the emotion is, who's involved, and what triggers it.

Step 3: Feel your body's response. A sucker punch may cause your heart to start racing suddenly, with even stronger emotions bubbling up inside you. Don't judge or suppress what you feel; by doing so, it causes emotional backup. Do you ever try to turn off happiness or gratitude? For now, feel, observe, laugh at it or talk to it.

Step 4: Let the emotion pass. Your body reacts to a situation based on how you interpret the impact of the person's behavior on you. When you experience an unpleasant event that's linked to your past, you go on the defensive. An internal dialogue ensues, and before you know it you're in so much turmoil it can cause an external outburst.

Have you ever been in a conversation with someone who says something you don't like? You mentally check out of the conversation and start tossing around thoughts about what the person could have meant. When you return to the conversation, you try to fill in the gap. Instead of holding onto the emotion and letting it occupy your mental space, let it pass through you. With self-reflection, you can revisit the comment to identify why it affected you the way that it did.

Step 5: Observe your response. Become the witness of your desired response to the person. When you think back on the situation, ask yourself: "What did I want to say? How did I want to say it? How would it have impacted my relationship?"

Step 6: Assess the issue. Think about why you felt the way that you did. Search for core answers.

In your journal, record the event to understand yourself and your triggers better.

Behavioral Trigger Tracking Example:

INQUIRY	ASSESSMENT
Situation	Told how to do my job.
Body Response	Body stiffens.
Feeling Response	Incompetence, rejection, disappointment.
Core Response	Not feeling trusted to handle the task.
Pain Point	Criticized for decisions and how tasks were completed growing up. Often told, "You don't listen."
Action Response	Anger, defensive, argumentative.
Truth of the Situation	The person is only expressing preferences.
Awareness	Being called stupid in the past makes me feel instruction is mistrust in my ability to get the job done effectively. Preferences aren't a personal attack on me or my work.

Strengthen critical decision-making skills. As you continue to purge past negative emotions, you'll gain more self-control that comes with greater accuracy when making decisions. As an executive leader, you make decisions that impact an entire organization and its constituents. Here are four steps to balance your thinking while increasing your critical decision-making competence and credibility:

1. **Remove yourself from the equation.** Acknowledge the situation isn't about you—it's for you. Whatever happens, it's an opportunity for you to demonstrate your intelligence and curiosity. By removing yourself from the situation, you'll be able to regroup and develop your plan of action quickly.

2. **Pinpoint what's really happening.** Most encounters have a lot of moving parts that are interconnected. For this reason, it can be challenging to determine where to focus your attention. Be open. Ask questions. Get to the core of the issue quickly.

3. **Build a strategy.** People want you to include them in the decision-making process, and they also want development and direction. Decide to be decisive.

4. **Focus on a resolution.** Decide that your target is to resolve the problem; otherwise, discussions about the problem will never end. This positions you as a trustworthy leader that people believe in and want to follow.

5. **Develop and follow the plan.** Once you decide on a course of action, lay it out, and execute. The key to showcasing executive presence is the poise, confidence, and calmness with which you go about doing your work.

Mind your manners; reflect maturity. People talk about each other. We often tell them what to say based on our interactions with them. I'm not referring to the people who gossip. I'm referring to people who share their experience while interacting with you. Mature leaders don't flaunt power; they share it. These are habits you can develop to become a leader with executive presence:

1. **Be an engaged listener.** Leaders look forward to ways to advance the organization. That's difficult to do when conversations focus on you. Developing executive presence requires you to listen and ask questions of others. Leaders provide space for people to create their own experience while interacting with them.

2. **Be measured when you speak.** Train yourself to think before you speak. Don't be the executive who communicates in the hallway with employees about issues that belong in the boardroom or a private setting. This behavior demonstrates an inability to model appropriate behavior.

3. **Position yourself wisely.** Executive presence doesn't mean you have to be stiff, but it does require you to be wise. Pictures are worth a thousand words. When asked to take selfies with employees train yourself to remain in the position you've been entrusted to hold. Position yourself and your body so that when the photo ends up on LinkedIn, Facebook, Instagram or elsewhere online, you've maintained your poise and integrity as an executive.

4. **Stay present**. Some CEOs and other workplaces are banning cellphones from meetings. This is partly because of a secret recording capability, but research indicates it's mostly due to inattentive employees. Having to take cellphones from adults should not be necessary, especially for those seeking to become an executive. Show up the way you'd like others to show up when you're presenting. Stay present and be engaged in meetings and when someone is talking.

5. **Practice conscious communication.** Remember, you're always communicating. What and how you communicate is a dead giveaway if you've reached executive presence. Use the tips I provided earlier to organize your thoughts for concise communication. Before you speak, take a breath and calmly share your thoughts while maintaining eye contact with your audience. If the pitch of your voice rises, it's asking a question even if you intend to make a statement.

6. **Use your internal tools, knowledge, and network.** Developing executive presence through self-actualizing doesn't mean you'll do everything correctly. Use all your resources to support yourself and others as you continuously evolve.

Executive presence isn't something that's out of your reach. It's actually rather simple. Treat people the way you want them to treat you, have discipline over yourself, and present yourself in a way that makes people want to be like you. Make sure your decisions are based on what's fair and in the best interest of everyone, and communicate your knowledge in a way that applies to the audience for which you are speaking. All this requires courage, confidence, and competence: qualities that become your standard way of doing business.

STEP 2

POSITION YOUR BRAND AND PRACTICE EXECUTIVE PRESENCE

THE DOORS FLY OPEN. An entrepreneur (or partners) walks down the hallway. As the small business owner enters "the tank," the sharks smile at the individual and focus on her appearance. Their eyes become fixated on the individual; it appears they are trying to read her. Regardless of what happens within the next 10 minutes, her life will change. The passage ends, and she's eyeball-to-eyeball with five billionaire investors. The entrepreneur is there seeking an investor and a partnership in exchange for a percentage of her company. But first, she has to pitch the sharks. I'm referring, of course, to the reality television show *Shark Tank*.

From my perspective, the show is as much about personal branding as it is business. The foundational strength of the entrepreneur's business is financial; however, other factors influence the decision of the investor. These factors are also key reasons people are swayed to hire, invest, and do business with you.

The entrepreneur introduces herself, and the pitch begins. Each person is different, but the more dynamic, conversational, and professional the entrepreneurs are, the more interest there is. After numbers are tossed around and the sharks decide they like the person, they'll inquire about her background. Justifying one's credentials and telling a personal story often gets a shark on the hook. One shark investor once said, "All the time I've been up here, I've never lost money on someone who deeply believes in what they're doing and sees something greater than just making a buck."

How personal branding influences an investor's decision is worthy of our attention, evaluation, and conversation. In this chapter you'll learn how to maximize opportunities, recognize what leaders are listening for, and position and pitch your package to become someone that captures leadership's attention.

Your Brand Position

You and your brand already have a position in the marketplace. And leadership has placed you in a player's lineup based on how you present yourself, apply your knowledge, and use your competencies. If you've made unconscious career moves in the past, now is the time to create a thoughtful, strategic plan. A blueprint won't make you inflexible; it will make you intentional. By designing a marketing plan with your anticipated goal in mind, you'll know which people, projects, and positions best align with your talents, temperament, and target.

Experience has taught me that some people become uncomfortable when I talk about positioning yourself and identifying people to target. A brand position plan for yourself and your career brings higher value to the people with whom you'll create alliances and the organization as a whole. Once you establish your plan, your job will be to courageously work it to advance yourself by helping others improve themselves. By implementing a plan of action, you'll profit by a surge in your visibility and credibility.

Your Brand Equity

Brand equity includes tangible and intangible assets that position you as an expert. It's what people come to expect from your brand based on your record, relationships, and reputation.

Intangible assets. Your intangible value comprises the experiences, expertise, and reputation that you leverage to influence others. When people can come to you to discuss a challenge, apply your advice, and get anticipated results—you become the go-to person in the workplace and the thought leader in the industry. Here's an example:

> In October 2017, I received an email with "possible book project" in the subject line. In part, it read, "I was excited to find your website in my research, as your coaching specialties align so well with this project. I love that you offer advice on leadership and relationships in the workplace that's results-oriented and actionable. I also was interested to learn that you wrote *Self-Esteem for Dummies*, along with several titles of your own, since the ability to convey your personal insight in writing doesn't come easily to everyone.

Your brand equity works precisely the same way. You share advice that people can use to solve their problems. It could be educational, financial, legal, or medical, or it could be the best way to connect with constituents, retain and develop employees, or align employee performance with profits. People start talking about you when they see results for themselves. Listen carefully to what they say because they'll tell you precisely what you can market. Use the information to position yourself as someone with specialized knowledge. This is how to develop and increase your brand's awareness. Brand awareness is people becoming aware of who you are, what you do, and the results you help them create.

Relationships. Your brand equity has political, economic, and social value, too. It's what gives you an edge. Confidence can be built, skills can be developed, customers can be served, but a strong network of solid relationships is, by far, the most valuable asset you have to raise the value of your brand. I'm not referring to followers on social media. I'm referring to the touch point you have with people you can call. When they see your name on the caller ID, they pick up.

Remember, human beings make decisions. When you have relationships, you learn the goings-on and inside secrets, and can position yourself accordingly. A conversation I had with a financial investor revealed how some people dangerously miss the point, causing an organization's brand to suffer. She said, "I don't care who I'm talking to; I treat everyone the same. Professional athletes come in here, and they expect me to know who they are. I don't care. I treat them the same way as I treat a janitor."

Her attitude is an example of the shift from business etiquette and high customer service to casual business comfort. It sounds honorable to say everyone is treated the same, but it's not good business. Here's why: Everyone has different needs. There should be a customer service standard, and every person should be treated with respect. Knowing your audience is good branding. Treating them in a way that makes them feel good about doing business with the organization is leveraging the brand, which is why the customer walked through your doors or visited your website. This concept is also applicable to your personal and professional relationships.

Executive presence is flexible and grants you the ability to make critical decisions on the spot. It adjusts to the needs of the person standing in front of you, without ever compromising your integrity. Building relationships and moving the customer experience from good to great drive up the stock of the organization.

Contribution. Your innovative ideas and intellectual property and your skills, talents, and abilities contribute to the revenue and growth of the organization. Throughout this book, you have spent a lot of time documenting what you can contribute to an organization, so I won't repeat it here. Just be sure to use what you've recorded to help you identify your marketplace position.

Positioning Your Contribution

A part of brand positioning is being able to make projections about industry changes and organizational shifts. In addition to executing your role, position yourself as a forward-thinking leader by foreseeing short- and long-term modifications necessary to the succession plan. Whether adjustments are needed in employee and client retention, reputation management, financial planning or any other area, never move ahead of leadership and start implementing changes on your own. Strategically discuss your perceptions and how you can help the organization with your sponsor. When you do this, you demonstrate offensive posturing, tremendous business insight, and attentiveness to the needs of the company.

I want to clarify the difference between a mentor and a sponsor. A mentor is a person who helps guide your career. This person provides advice to help you identify areas of opportunity to grow your career. A sponsor goes to bat for you.

For instance, when it's time to decide on the next power broker to be invited to the boardroom, a sponsor wears your T-shirt. Here's how it often happens: The influencers, #bigbosses, sit around the table and propose names of people who the leadership team has been watching for a while. When your name is announced, your sponsor speaks up and endorses your character and capital. Human capital includes your communication, critical decision-making, and management skills. Your brand equity is your experience and any specialized knowledge or ability you have. Together, these tangible and intangible brand assets that you possess increase your credibility and value to the organization and its internal and external constituents.

Everyone at the table knows there's a lot at stake as they persuasively advocate for their favorite candidate for the position. These meetings can sometimes come down to a dogfight between influencers who also lend their brand equity, human capital, and political clout to pull you through the process and to success.

If you are eyeing a position or you are on the path to the C-suite, you have the most significant role to play in getting yourself there. In addition to a stellar performance record, you have to nurture relationships with key stakeholders—employees, customers, board members, and stockholders—whenever possible. When you think about positioning yourself, be wise, be strategic and think outside the box, but stay within the borders of the unwritten rules.

Building Trust for Brand Positioning

Most people can tell you that trust is built on openness, honesty, integrity, transparency, listening, communicating, and understanding. It's also about responding to the needs of the person or group you've committed to building trust. Knowing something logically doesn't equate with knowing how to do it or having the maturity to do it. It can be a situation that you perceive as insignificant. What you do is a small thing to you, but the outcome of your decision makes a big difference in how a person perceives, trusts, and engages with you in the future.

Some character flaws are too close for comfort, and management prefers not to discuss those with you. So they don't. You're left without an explanation as to why your career growth suddenly became stagnate. Case in point, when management asks you a direct question, you respond with an indirect answer. Your response makes a person think you're hiding something or being evasive, violating one of the core competencies to building trust. If you can't share something, tell the person that you're not at liberty to share at this time; that's being honest and honorable. It's then up to the person to do what they want with your response.

Companies can't afford to take risks they may have taken before the age of social media. Leaders know they are under the watchful eye of groups and individuals that can call their hand on improprieties that once went unchallenged. You know right from wrong, so color within the lines of integrity, and you'll be fine, especially when dealing with issues of appropriateness. If you're unsure about an issue, talk with your mentor or someone else you trust.

Brand Positioning for Transition, Transformation, and Change

Takeovers, mergers, market movement, and new leadership can come in a wave, storm, or tsunami. When it happens, decide whether the direction of the company is still a good fit for you. Most companies in transition will want to minimize the loss of valued employees, but they know everyone isn't built for unstable, turbulent environments that transition often creates. If you decide to stay, position yourself so that leadership can see your commitment, stability, and faith in them and the organization. This is how to navigate change, position yourself, practice executive presence, and increase your brand's value:

Keep your eyes on your target. During drastic change, transition, and transformation, it's typical to feel as though you don't know what your next step should be. It's traumatizing to feel disconnected, vulnerable, and at risk of losing your job and all that you've invested. Decide on your target and keep your eyes on it.

Know the focus of the organization. We are creatures of habit, but change is upon us. The people, the rules, and the system are in the midst of transformation. What you've done over the last 20 years isn't necessarily needed for the next 20 years. It doesn't align with the new paradigm. Remember, when you were hired you were a part of the team who implemented a new way of doing business. Organizational change isn't personal; it's a deliberate attempt to keep the company relevant and competitive in the marketplace.

Staying in the past will only frustrate leadership and cause you to sabotage your career. Ask questions to understand why the leadership team believes the decisions they're making are necessary. As best you can, stay out of the emotional pit, and put what you hear into context so that you see where you are, where they want to go, and how you can help them get there.

Realign your brand. Based on what you learn by being attentive, asking questions, and realigning your brand, here are some foundational basics: During a transition, company leaders work to strengthen the infrastructure by streamlining processes, increasing efficiencies, and managing the negative impact of change. Leadership will tell you what they can when they can so remain alert and agile by keeping the following in mind:

Minimize distractions. Rumors will fly, and the volume of the noise will rise. Dial into your frequency, and find your guiding light. You may be on a need-to-know basis until leadership has a clear understanding of its strengths, weaknesses, opportunities, and threats. Don't spend time on anything that doesn't work for your benefit.

Control what you can control. Focus on what you're accountable for each day and deliver. You'll have strategic goals to meet. Push hard, meet the objectives, and the rest will take care of itself.

Brand positioning allows you to control your narrative. According to an article in USA Today, among the most common and up-to-date phrases in business, politics, and savvy American life is "'controlling the narrative.' That is, telling it your way before someone else gets to tell it—and possibly tell it better—their way." The way you show up and what you say when you do, determines what people hear and respond to—even if you don't whisper one word.

STOP BEFORE YOU TAKE ANOTHER STEP!

Social Media Marketing

When I was looking for an assistant, I received a well-written email response to my inquiry. Attached was an equally impressive resume; I googled the applicant. What I discovered didn't match the brand of my company—at all. The profile and photograph were disturbing. Curious about what other companies do in this situation, I clicked the Chrome icon.

According to the job search site CareerBuilder, in 2018, 70 percent of employers screened candidates on social media before making a hiring decision, and 43 percent of them used social media to check on their employees. I recently read that 78 percent of workers meet a new hire online first.

The workplace, partnerships, and community boards are platforms where you choose to participate to increase your visibility and share your intellectual property. Facebook, LinkedIn, Twitter, and other social media platforms are tools you use to boost your brand and expand your brand's value.

A Compelling Reason to Say Yes

You're among hundreds of thousands of people who work in the same industry. For the most part, you are one of the thousands who can satisfy the need of your audiences. So why would they choose you?

Could it be your standout skills, talent, and abilities? Is it your professional attire that gives you the edge? Or, does your communication style give you an advantage? The number one reason people make it to the top of their industry isn't because they are the best. It's because they have mastered how to package, position, and promote their value better than anyone else vying for the same job or contract.

Entrepreneurs and employees who assume the answer is yes and then don't adequately prepare for questions are stunned by the brilliance of conscious business people. It's insulting to a person with whom you have a meeting that you would not take 10 minutes to learn one or two things about them—especially when all it takes is a quick online search.

When you don't sufficiently plan to speak with industry or organizational leaders, it communicates amateurish, presumptuous, and unbusinesslike behavior. If you prepare as though you expect the answer to be no, then you'll be better prepared to craft a compelling reason for the person to say yes.

Careless Small Talk

Positioning yourself isn't just about the next job you want; it's also about how you strategically target leadership and engage in stimulating conversation that makes you memorable. Whether by accident or deliberate positioning, an opportunity to make yourself known to leadership can change the course of your career—unless you don't know what to say. An executive once shared with me that one of the most disappointing moments is when you're talking to one of your bright, young leaders who represents the future of the company and has no idea how to maximize the moment.

You can avoid this from happening by doing what senior leaders do—read the company's annual report, newsletter, and attend networking events. Most organizations have Facebook pages, and some CEOs provide updates on YouTube about company matters. Always be prepared to have a conversation about the company, competition, or an interesting problem the company is facing that that has gained some success.

Protect Your Mind from Research

Research is essential to help us understand our challenges and devise a plan to fix them. Most certainly, it has its rightful place. However, with regard to how people view those from different backgrounds, if you rely on statistics that tell you all the things that can go wrong, it can hinder you from taking chances on yourself that could go right. You'll begin to believe and look for the biases versus the moments that can take your career higher.

For example, research indicates women of color have less latitude than white women. Women have more to prove than white men, and men in general. If you don't wear makeup, you're not trustworthy. The point is this: If you're not prepared, poised, polished, and well put together—woman or man—you don't look the part of an executive, nor are you ready to be one.

I'm not foolish enough to think that biases and discrimination are nonexistent. Like many people, I've experienced it myself. But they didn't come only from one group of people—I've experienced it from men and women alike, and color has no boundaries. And although not intentional, I have my challenges to overcome when it comes to having a preconceived notion about a person based on how they act, speak, and look. I bet you have yours, too.

Fortunately, the 21st century has ushered in new awareness and changes. According to Wikipedia, women have been elected from 46 out of the 50 states to the U.S. House of Representatives. And, there are top companies for women and women with children to work. More than ever, there are conversations about diversity and inclusion, and a real effort and actions are being taken to bring about a change.

We all have a part to play in this much-needed work of shifting what we define as the appearance of competency. That work starts within by knowing yourself and becoming more open-minded. We are in a better place. If we continue to rehash the past and repeat the same rhetoric, we'll fail to embrace the progress we're making. It's difficult to keep looking back and still move forward. I encourage you to forge ahead as if there aren't any barriers, and if you bump into one, know that you are courageous, confident, and competent enough to find your way around it—as so many great people have done before us.

THE PLAN TO POSITION YOUR BRAND

You have the information you need to position your brand. How does it line up with the organization where you work or want to serve? Where are the gaps in the organization? Can your expertise assist in bridging one or more of these gaps? Who needs to know about your abilities? How can you tell your stories about your skills and to whom?

Follow the steps to create a plan that works in sync with the needs of the organization. Start with a new sheet of paper.

Step 1: Write down your ultimate goal.

Step 2: Read the most recent annual report of the organization. It will give you a lot of insight into where the company is, where it's going, and any areas of risk. This is invaluable information in identifying where your expertise fits, and where to target your brand equity. Once you have a clear understanding of how you and the organization are in alignment, write down your mission statement. Next to your mission statement, document what specific challenges the organization is facing and what department is working on a solution.

Step 3: Identify and list the audiences directly impacted by the problem. Then list the names of decision-makers who are responsible for solving it.

Step 4: Get clear on the values of the organization. How are the values described in the careers section of the organization's website? How do employees view them? Are the values reflected in the leadership's decisions? Document your findings. It's essential you accurately read the social and political landscape. Next, spend time observing people and how they make decisions. Ask questions in a manner that don't turn the conversation into a gossip session. Consider opening statements such as "Help me understand…" or, "Can you tell me why?" The purpose of the discussion is to advance your career, not damage your brand. Record what you learn. Refer to the Mind Elevation: My Essentials, which lists your priorities. Do your values and those of the organization interconnect? If so, make a list of the similarities. You want to bring your personality traits, values, and priorities forward that most align with the organization's values and culture.

Step 5: Document the company's tagline. What is your brand story or motto? Identify and document how they intersect. When asking questions or sharing your expertise, you want to always refer back to the values and brand of the organization. This is especially important because it justifies your ideas, and your colleagues will find it difficult to argue with the company's values and brand. It takes the emphasis off you and puts the attention on the purpose of the organization.

Step 6: Bring forward your area of expertise, the department you identified in step 2, and the people you identified in step 3.

Step 7: Spend time observing the people with whom you want to work. Identify the ones looking for opportunities to connect with the next tier of leaders. Refer to your earlier list of people who are in your network. Seek out the people you know you'll need to communicate with to assist you as you posture yourself for new opportunities. Make them aware of what you want to achieve. Thanks to the research you did earlier in this process, you're prepared to articulate concisely what you need and how these individuals can help you.

Step 8: Once you've developed your plan, keep it close by. You'll want to pull out data that focuses your attention on your primary target. Here's an example:

AUDIENCE	EXPERTISE	NAME OF CONTACT
Chief of Marketing	Analyzing consumer behavior. Developing compelling stories to connect customers with the company's brand.	Person N. Charge

STEP 3

PROMOTE YOUR BRAND AND PRESENT EXECUTIVE PRESENCE

SHOULD I USE SOCIAL MEDIA, build a website and blog, or submit articles to the company newsletter? That's the most frequently asked question I get from clients. Success leaves clues, but there isn't a cookie cutter solution to promoting and positioning your brand. It's your brand. You have personal goals and professional aspirations for yourself and your career. You have a unique personality that powerfully communicates your brilliance. Your passions are exclusively yours, and your pattern of showing up in the world is marked with your footsteps and fingerprints.

The moment you opened this book, you began to discover hidden treasures within you. In Chapter 1, you pinpointed where you are, what you have, and how to navigate the internal barriers that once blurred your vision of yourself and your ability to succeed. Chapter 2 led you on a journey to assess and transcend your current brand.

In Step One, Package Your Brand and Develop Executive Presence—the core of the brand and executive presence development process—we unlocked the seven components of branding. You began to adjust your communication style, recreate your image, and develop the posture and poise that captures the attention of your audience. I can only imagine the buzz created as a result of the style and behavioral changes that better reflect you.

Step Two, Position Your Brand and Practice Executive Presence, unveiled the unique contributions you're capable of bringing to an organization. You developed a plan to guide your thinking in how to position yourself as a problem solver. You discovered that change isn't a personal attack on you; instead, it's an opportunity being granted for you to practice executive presence. Now, you may wonder, what do I do with all my greatness? My response: Share it.

Step Three, Promote Your Brand and Present Executive Presence is about strategic implementation. How do you combine everything that you've learned to promote your brand and advance your career? In this step, you'll gain more know-how on positioning and promoting your brand and presenting like an executive. You'll get the wisdom you need to optimize moments that help you become the expert at the table, the go-to person in the company, or whatever you desire and wherever your brand takes you.

Develop a Marketing Mind

By following the steps to package yourself and develop your executive presence, you're in a position to make a good impression. Before you launch, you have to decide which are the best platforms to get your audience's attention. It begins with understanding that in general, like you, people are thinking about their advancement and how others are perceiving them. They want to grow their brand equity and their human capital. That requires having the right people around them at the right time. You could be the person they're looking for; you just have to be in a position for them to notice you.

Developing a marketing mind will help you. If you pay attention to television, radio, billboard, and magazine advertisements, you'll begin to understand how the best marketers in the world tap into the minds of their audiences. This understanding will help you gain perspective on how your audiences think and respond to what they hear, see, and feel. A huge part of getting a person to notice you is paying attention to their behavior. We're always expressing ourselves, even when we don't know it.

Giving people what they want makes you likable. Satisfying their needs makes you marketable. Getting them tangible results makes you credible. Here's my three-step process for getting and holding a person's attention:

Step 1: Be likable. Giving people what they want is what makes people like you. Oprah explains it best. She said: "There is a common denominator in the human experience that we all share. We all want to know that what we do, and what we say, and who we are matters. We want to be validated."

Regardless of how successful the person is that you want to reach, that person wants to know what he or she does matters. I want to caution you though. Disingenuous comments will be detected. If, however, you approach the person with sincere compliments about what you've learned from them, how they inspired you, or how you've been able to advance your personal or professional development as a result of something they said or did, you will be memorable.

I've discovered this: Most people will start with a compliment and then immediately make it about them. For instance, "I really admire you, and I want to be like you. Will you mentor me?" Anything like that or a knockoff of that tactic is a turnoff. That is not the way to build a relationship and inspire engagement. Nor is, "Your tip last week in the meeting really inspired me to become a better leader. I'd love to work for you someday."

Consider this:

I appreciate the suggestion you offered in the meeting last week regarding how to better manage time by delegating tasks to team members and scheduling weekly accountability calls. I implemented that idea the day after you shared it. I've noticed fewer interruptions, and my productivity has nearly doubled. Thank you!

Undoubtedly, there is a noticeable difference in what you often say or hear and suggestions shared. You didn't directly sell yourself. However, you framed it in a way that shares a lot about yourself while complimenting them. Here's what the person now knows about you:

- You appreciate them.
- You listen.
- You act on good advice.
- You assess results.
- You give credit for your success.

You've just planted your first "Wow!" seed.

Step 2: Be marketable. You've given them what they want by communicating they matter. Now, satisfy their need. Operate from the premise that everyone has a set of priorities, and your job is to find ways to support that. Based on the reaction, they will appreciate your attentiveness and gratitude for their help.

The next step is to build the relationship by giving them something of value. Most people love good publicity. Decide how and where you want to share the story. You can share it in the next business meeting, in the company's newsletter, or an email. If it's in written form, get it edited.

My public relations background tells me that you'd be well advised to email the article to the person for review before submitting it for publication. This allows them to add anything that you may have missed, and most importantly, the gesture communicates respect. You'd say something like:

"Hi, Kim. I've continued to use the time management strategy you proposed, and the results are phenomenal. It has worked so well for me that I thought other leaders in the company could benefit from your advice. I want to submit the attached article, "Take Back Your Time," for publication in the company newsletter. Since I included your name in the article, I wanted to run it by you first. The deadline for submission is June 1, two weeks from today. Please confirm it's okay to share your story. Thanks again for your leadership."

This strategy continues to build the relationship by increasing the number of touch points. The published article will increase the person's credibility—and your visibility. Now, within only 30 days, you're on her radar. Here's what this communicates about you:

- You're thoughtful.
- You're respectful.
- You're helpful.
- You care about others.
- You work in the best interest of the company.
- You like to share what works.
- You genuinely appreciated the suggestion.
- Your thinking is next level.

Step 3: Be credible. You have the person's attention. They like you and have a sense that they know what kind of person you are. Next, you have to confirm that they can trust you. Regardless of how much buzz is created from the article, direct the attention back to the person. By pushing the focus toward the person, it affirms your integrity and signals your good intentions. No one likes to feel taken advantage of, even though your visibility increased immensely. If you get significant feedback, or a personal email from leadership, use it as an opportunity to meet the person for coffee or lunch. Here's what you can say:

"Hi, Kim: Responses from the article have been amazing! If you're open, I want to share the feedback with you. Do you have time in the next few weeks to meet for lunch?"

Here's what this will do for you:

- Build trust.
- Increase interest.
- Showcase your character.
- Create opportunity.
- Expand your brand.
- Forge an ally.

When you have a face-to-face meeting, do not pitch the person unless she asks you what you want. The purpose is to continue to build trust by demonstrating that you can effectively communicate. That starts with listening. Most executives I've been around are savvy listeners and will immediately start asking you questions, so be prepared. Most often the character-based questions will be presented casually. You'll feel like you're talking to a close friend. Follow their lead, but don't get too comfortable. Stay in your brand and project your calm, confident executive presence. You'll want to make sure that everything you say refers back to what they want to achieve based on the organization's goals. Keep this point in mind even when communicating what you want. Don't forget to relax and share your passion and personality.

Go Where They Are, Build Your Career Where You Are

In 2013, I received a call to launch an online speakers program. It included Jack Canfield, best-selling co-author of the Chicken Soup for the Soul series, and four other national speakers. The call came three years after I had completed a one-year business development program with Bradley Communications Corp. The investment gave me face-to-face contact with the owners of the company four times that year.

How did they remember me years later out of hundreds of people? One of the owners puts it this way, "She's memorable—unforgettable." Am I really? Or is it that I have a keen understanding of what Oprah said about what people want? Whenever I had a few moments to talk with the owners, I'd share how a strategy I learned through the program helped my business to expand. I believe he remembered how every conversation we had made him feel good about the work he was doing to help others. In addition to helping to build an online training program and promotional materials, the company hired me to coach their clients.

You can connect with your audience through conferences, company events, a company newsletter, presenting a webinar or other type of training, volunteering, and social media. There are three key points to keep in mind:

Prepare for unexpected conversations. Don't walk up to a senior leader with nothing to say. It's likely the leader will either go silent after friendly greetings or will engage in courteous small talk about what you do. You want to move beyond that, to initiate a more in-depth conversation. When you do your homework daily, it'll be easy to find a connection point, and it can grow from there. For example, I had a meeting at a client's office. I was waiting for the elevator to go up. When the door opened, the CEO and his assistant walked off. I noticed him immediately and introduced myself. I shared excerpts from one of his speeches and the impact it had on me. He smiled broadly and expressed his gratitude. As he walked away, I overheard him ask his assistant, "Who is that? What does she do?"

Whet their appetite. Strategically share your success from a value-proposition perspective. It should pique the interest of your contact just enough to make the person want to know more. The only reason to want to know more about you is to blaze a trail back to them. Let's say you're speaking with an executive about talent. He expresses concern about retention. First, engage him by getting his thoughts on the issue and how he would resolve it. Listen attentively and respond based on what you hear. Here's a suggestive follow-up statement: "I can appreciate what you're saying because when I worked for ABC Company, we had some of the same issues. We implemented a strategy that increased our retention rate to 97 percent. It sounds like you're on point." You can't fake it; you must be prepared to answer any questions he may have on the spot. Now, you've positioned yourself as an expert.

Stay on your path. I'm advising you to connect with leaders, identify their agenda, and find ways to help them elevate their success. What I'm not suggesting you do is abandon your target and aim your arrow at theirs. That's not what positioning and promoting yourself is about. Unless there's an agreement that if you redirect your focus from your goal to theirs, you'll receive your fair value and compensation; every decision you make should lead you to hit your target.

Seek Mutual Partnership Opportunities

It's vital to build alliances and create partnerships that are substantial, influential, and mutual to keep your career or business on a continuous incline. Any partnership you consider should be significant for your growth and theirs, the scope of your influence and network should expand, and there must be mutual value.

I followed this strategy as an employee, and I continue to use it in my business today. My first partnership was with Dr. Randal Pinkett, who I met at an event where we were both speaking. He's the co-founder, chairman, and CEO of BCT Partners, multimillion-dollar management, technology, and policy consultancy. You may remember him as the Season 4 winner of *The Apprentice*. The goal was to collaborate with a powerhouse name for added credibility while diversifying my portfolio. In return, Randal added a reliable brand to his team of trainers.

Years later, I accepted a contract to become a faculty member with Bradley Communications Corp. At the time, their email list of more than 65,000 speakers and writers substantially increased my brand's visibility. For five years, I coached hundreds of Bradley's clients and helped get the results the company was seeking. I received compensation and exposure that led to my first book deal. Bradley got a bankable brand that helped grow and diversify the company's client base.

In 2018, I decided my business was moving in a different direction. Four months later, I linked up with the Society for Human Resources Management (SHRM), which, I understand, has more than 300,000 members. I'm a member of SHRM's Speakers Bureau, giving presentations at the group's conferences; we also have conversations about how to make workplaces better while serving their membership.

I want to point out some specifics about this strategic model. The points shared here will help you in your day-to-day interactions and thought processes as you identify people or organizations to build alliances with and develop partnerships.

Find the Right Partnerships

Questions about how to partner and with whom to partner are common concerns of clients. It's essential to be diligent when looking for alliances and partnerships. Who you tie your brand to is as critical a decision as to whom you choose to be a member of your inner circle. Here's how I'd advise you to choose:

Check the brand. When you attach your brand to another person's brand or that of an organization, you want to make sure that their brand is worth bragging about. That's what partnerships and alliances are—people endorsing one another and influencing the direction of each other's career. At the very least, you will be tied to one another through social media, publicity, public appearances, serving business clients, and more. Check behind the brand to ensure the person's character aligns with the brand image. As an employee, this is extremely important. Note: It's harder to detach yourself or rebuild your brand if you're part of a small community.

Begin with the end in mind. You develop strong ties to people you choose to create alliances or partnerships. At some point, your business relationship may look different than when you started; you may discontinue engagement. You'll want to dissolve the collaboration respectfully, yet remain good colleagues. Before you enter into the relationship, can you see how they will likely interact with you and handle situations?

For instance, I met an Olympic goal medalist on LinkedIn. Based on his background, I thought it would be a good fit for us to partner on a project. We scheduled our first meeting, and he was late. He said it was due to a prior meeting. It seemed we had a good connection during our initial conversation, and decided to schedule our next conversation. He was late for our second meeting as well. After the meeting was over, he asked to plan our third meeting. I declined. It was apparent to me his style of doing business would only frustrate me. My point: Pay attention to what people do. If they are late for meetings with you, they'll be late for meetings with clients. People have perceptions of themselves and others. When they respect you, you'll see it in their behavior. From dealing with countless clients, I've learned this: Raggedy on the front end equals raggedy on the back end!

Grow the partnership gradually. You have goals and objectives. When you transmit desperation, people will detect it and will take advantage of you. People don't shoot to the top of an industry overnight. Slowly build your brand, and as you do, it will gain momentum and attract interest. Having a track record of continuous growth and success signals that you're likable, marketable, and credible. Elevating your brand to this level will help catch the attention of people of the same caliber. When you decide to partner, agree to one project at a time. As you see how they operate and vice versa, you'll be able to make a more informed decision about the relationship.

Know what you need. Know what you want out of any partnership, and be able to articulate it. However, it may not be easy to identify the opportunities a person or platform may bring to a collaboration with you. Think about your brand and what it needs. You may not get compensation for working on a particular project at work, but you'll gain visibility and the opportunity to grow your credibility. Partnerships can come from people within the organization or industry. They might come, for instance, from media, educational institutions, social media influencers, nonprofits, and colleagues.

Grow first. Before there's ever a partnership offer, there's a reputable, relevant well-packaged brand. Continue to build your brand, and people will want to partner with you.

PARTNERSHIP POSSIBILITIES

Who would you like to create an alliance with to advance your career? Joining forces can accelerate your career. Is there a balance in the brand equity of each partner to generate interest in joining forces? Review the example below to see how to evaluate partnering with someone, then choose the people or organizations that interest you:

Potential Partner	His Value Proposition	Value of Partnering	Downside to Partnership
Juan	Strong brand presence, excellent writing skills, creative, thinks out the box, well liked	Leverage networks, strong skills for online brand expansion, could mentor him	Lacks executive presence

Your Growth Plan

When you enjoy your job, you may be tempted to sustain your workplace position. That's the path to disaster. Brands that survive the shifting marketplace know that how their audiences think and see themselves in the world changes—sometimes daily. The market movement is so fast that some leaders find it challenging to keep up with the changes. That's where you come in. Follow these steps to stay connected with your market.

- Listen to your audience.
- Give your audience what they want.
- Serve your audience.
- Stay connected with your audience.
- Continuously reinvent yourself and expand your brand.

Another part of your growth plan should include how you're going to manage your brand through growth, evolution, and elevation. The process doesn't change; the players do. Use these critical areas as focal points to stay relevant:

Your innovative ideas. Stay on top of your game by finding creative new ways to help others get what they want.

Your intellectual property. Look for new experiences that challenge you and grow your knowledge, skills, and abilities. If you commit to continuously evolving, you'll always have value and opportunities that will take you to the next level of achievement. Consider the following options for professional growth:

- Attend seminars, conferences, and webinars
- Listen to podcasts
- Read books
- Earn a certification
- Earn an advanced degree

- Hire a coach
- Join a mastermind group
- Join a group coaching program
- Take an online course
- Volunteer

Your value proposition. Keep your audiences informed of what you're learning by sharing. Position your advice to show how it benefits them.

Your brand promise performance. Hit the target. Peak performance is what keeps you on your audience's radar, and it grows your likability, marketability, and credibility.

You now have the plan for personal brand and executive presence development. You have to step up, work it, refused to be denied, be innovative, and adjust accordingly—you can do it!

I wish you well on your journey to your next big contract, leadership opportunity, the C-suite or wherever your path takes you. It will not be a straight shot to the top. You'll have moments of bloopers and blunders, but don't lose sight of the target. Continue to mature your brand and add value to the organization where you work. Return to this resource when you need it, and I'll be there to support you as you give your brand and executive presence the boost it needs to elevate your life and career.

As always, there is more inside.

RESOURCES

Bradley Communications Corp., steveharrison.com. Marketing, communications, and business-development company for speakers and authors. (Accessed May 11, 2019)

Eckard Tolle, *A New Earth: Awakening to Your Life's Purpose* (Published August 29th 2006 by Plume) eckharttolle.com. Spiritual Teacher and Author. (Accessed May 11, 2019)

Lisa Nichols, *Abundance Now: Amplify Your Life and Achieve Prosperity Today* (Published January 5th 2016 by Dey Street Books) motivatingthemass.com; Founder and Chief Executive Officer of Motivating the Masses, Inc. (Accessed May 11, 2019)

Dr. Randal Pinkett, randalpinkett.com. Entrepreneur, speaker, community servant, author, campus CEO. Currently, co-founder, chairman, and CEO of his fifth venture, BCT Partners, a multimillion-dollar research, training, consulting, technology, and analytics firm based in Newark, New Jersey.

SHRM, Society for Human Resource Management, shrm.org.

S. Renee Smith, srenee.com. Provides free self-development tips, tools, and strategies to help boost self-esteem, build brands, and communicate effectively. S. Renee has produced more than 200 free videos on YouTube (https://www.youtube.com/user/sreneesmith) and online self-development programs (https://coachsrenee.com).

S. Renee Smith, *5 Steps to Assertiveness: How to Communicate with Confidence and Get What You Want* (Emeryville, California: Callisto Media, 2018). Distills into five easy-to-follow steps what S. Renee Smith has learned and taught about assertive communication.

S. Renee Smith, *There Is More Inside: Personal Essentials Needed for Living a Power-Packed Life* (Washington, D.C.: SRS Productions, Inc., 2005).

S. Renee Smith, *The Bridge to Your Brand: Likability, Marketability, Credibility* (Washington, D.C.: (SRS) Productions, Inc., 2011).

S. Renee Smith and Vivian Harte, *Self-Esteem for Dummies* (Hoboken, New Jersey: Wiley, 2015). Provides clear and innovative methods to help anyone behave with more self-assurance.

REFERENCES

Barbizon International, barbizonmodeling.com.

Beckwith, Dr. Michael Bernard, michaelbernardbeckwith.com. *Spiritual Liberation: Fulfilling Your Soul Purpose.* Founder and Director of Agape International Spiritual Center. (Accessed May 11, 2019)

CareerBuilder, press.careerbuilder.com/2017-06-15-Number-of-Employers-Using-Social-Media-to-Screen-Candidates-at-All-Time-High-Finds-Latest-CareerBuilder-Study (June 2017)

Carr, Dr. Kwame, *Turnaround Principles for Turnaround Principals: Protocols for Creating a Culture of Student Achievement* 2014 (CreateSpace, 2014). (Accessed May 11, 2019)

Hewlett, Sylvia Ann, *Executive Presence: The Missing Link Between Merit and Success* (New York: HarperBusiness, 2014). (Accessed May 11, 2019)

Mitchell, Charles, CNBC contributor. "CEOs are worried about three things this year—and No. 1 is whether you plan to quit," *Make It* cnbc.com/amp/2019/01/28/the-3-biggest-challenges-facing-ceos-in-2019-and-how-to-solve-them.html (January 28, 2019). (Accessed May 11, 2019)

Pitts, Byron, *Step Out on Nothing: How Faith and Family Helped Me Conquer Life's* Challenges (New York: St. Martin's Press, 2010).

Shark Tank, abc.go.com/shows/shark-tank

Sherman, Dr. Audrey, *"Dysfunction Interrupted: How to Quickly Overcome Depression and Anxiety, Starting Now,"* 2015. dysfunctioninterrupted.com (Accessed May 11, 2019)

Smith, S. Renee & Vivian Harte, *Self-Esteem for Dummies.* (New York: For Dummies, 2015).

Smith, S. Renee, *There Is More Inside: Personal Essentials Needed to Living a Power-Packed Life* (**Washington, D.C.: SRS Productions, Inc., 2005**).

Smith, S. Renee, *The Bridge to Your Brand: Likability, Marketability, Credibility* (**Washington, D.C.:** SRS Productions, Inc., 2011).

Smith, S. Renee, *5 Steps to Assertiveness: How to Communicate with Confidence and Get What You Want* (California: Althea Press, 2018).

Williams, Pharrell, Happy (New York City: Columbia Records, 2013).

Winfrey, Oprah, "The Oprah Winfrey Show Finale." Oprah.com. oprah.com /oprahshow/the-oprah-winfrey-show-finale_1/7. May 11, 2019.

The Conference Board, conference-board.org.

ACKNOWLEDGMENTS

While writing this book, my journey of uncovering more of my courage, confidence, and competence continued. I'm thankful for the lessons and the opportunity to share my life and knowledge with you.

This book grew out of my desire to be true to my brand. When booked to speak at the Society for Human Resource Management's annual conference, my first book on brand development, *The Bridge to Your Brand: Likability, Marketability, Credibility*, was one of the resources chosen to help develop SHRM's members. Written in 2011, *The Bridge*, although still relevant, doesn't reflect my current body of knowledge on personal brand development and executive presence. For this reason, on March 18, 2019, at 7:28 p.m., my fingers starting dancing across the keyboard—again, just 10 months after the release of *5 Steps to Assertiveness*.

It's been a privilege to put my comprehensive program in a book that will transform careers and workplaces around the world. This would not have happened at this time if Stephney Riley hadn't introduced me to Jeaneen Andrews-Feldman. When Jeaneen and I met, there was an instant connection, and she introduced me to the SHRM family. For both of these women, I am thankful.

HL Larry, you travelled this journey with me again. Thank you for your patience, insight, and time. Most important, thank you for taking care of me during long grueling hours.

My deepest gratitude is to God in whom I put my complete trust. To those who have chosen to take this beautiful, but sometimes challenging journey with me daily, I have endless appreciation for your love, support, and prayers: my husband, HL Larry; my parents, William J. and Shirley

M. Smith, Sr.; my best friend, Kirra Streat; my brother, Joseph Smith; and my aunt, Joan Draine-Burris. And to the rest of my siblings and large, extended family, you know who you are. Thank you!

ABOUT THE AUTHOR

S. Renee Smith is a renowned self-esteem and branding expert, life and business coach, and resource to the media. She has worked with over 100 clients in nine different industries and is sought after for her ability to shatter old beliefs and mental constructs—closing the gaps in the minds of audiences regarding how they see themselves, their careers, and their abilities to achieve success.

With more than 20 years of experience in communications, she has served as a television talk show host, producer, and spokesperson (United Paramount Network, Philadelphia), director of public relations at an academic institution, a corporate marketing representative, and a manager.

Her insights have been featured in *Entrepreneur*, *Shape*, *Woman's World*, and other magazines, and on *Marketing Daily* and many other websites. Plus, she has made countless radio and television appearances.

S. Renee is the author of four popular books: *There Is More Inside: Personal Essentials Needed for Living a Power-Packed Life*, *The Bridge to Your Brand: Likability, Marketability, Credibility*, *Our Hearts Wonder: Prayers to Heal Your Heart and Calm Your Soul*, and 5 Steps to *Assertiveness: How to Communicate with Confidence and Get What You Want*. She is also the co-author of *Self-Esteem for Dummies*, which was written for the world's best-selling "Dummies" reference brand series.